131096F

Presented to Roger Coates of Preston
Polytechnic Students Union 1978-79 in
appreciation of his support and interest
in the Lancashire Association of Trades
Councils.

C. Platt. President Lancs. C.A.T.C.
with Best Wishes for the future,

The Activist's Handbook

Trade Union Industrial Studies

This series makes two new types of provision in the area of industrial relations: first it is specifically directed to the needs of active trade unionists who want to equip themselves to be more effective, and second, the books are linked together in a series related to the requirements of existing training and education courses.

The books have been designed by a Curriculum Development Group drawn from the Society of Industrial Tutors: Michael Barratt Brown, Ed Coker, Bob Houlton, Ossie O'Brien and Geoffrey Stuttard, together with Charles Clark and Francis Bennett of the Hutchinson Publishing Group. The Curriculum Development Group has prepared the guidelines for the texts and edited them so that they form a complete set of teaching material for tutors and students primarily for use on trade union courses.

The texts are issued in sets of four, together with an accompanying resource book which provides additional background material for tutors and students.

Trade Union Industrial Studies

This series is published in three sets, each consisting of four student texts and an accompanying resource book. This book includes additional teaching material for tutors and students, a recommended list of books and a further exploration of the subjects by the authors of the texts.

Bob Houlton

The Activist's Handbook

A Guide to Organizing
and Communication

Hutchinson
in association with the
Society of Industrial Tutors

'It is a question first of all of discovering what one really is, what one's feelings really are, and then making allowance for the inevitable bias.'

(George Orwell, *The Decline of the English Murder and Other Essays*)

To Our Gerard

Hutchinson & Co (Publishers) Ltd
3 Fitzroy Square, London W1

London Melbourne Sydney Auckland
Wellington Johannesburg Cape Town
and agencies throughout the world

First published 1975
© Bob Houlton 1975

Filmset in Monophoto Times
by BAS Printers Ltd, Wallop, Hampshire
Printed in Great Britain by The Anchor Press Ltd
and bound by Wm Brendon & Son Ltd
both of Tiptree, Essex

ISBN 0 09 122600 7

Contents

Section I   Why . . . ?

This book is for activists:

* Men and women running voluntary organizations.
* Shop stewards and convenors fighting for justice at work.
* Branch secretaries, chairmen and committee-men.
* Political workers who meet, organize, canvass and help democracy survive.

My aims are modest. I hope that this book will provide a firm foundation upon which an activist can base his operations. It offers ways of examining and overcoming the doubts and uncertainties which always come with the job. The book uses research findings which have for a long time been available to professional manipulators. But it is also based on the numerous mistakes that I have made over the years as an activist. I hope this mixture of research findings and personal disasters will, in the end, help to swing the balance back to 'our side'.

---

1. A Little Blunder

Introduction

Everyone has memories that make him wince. We have all been in situations we would prefer to forget about. Surely you've been out on a Saturday night when someone has shouted across the room, 'Now, what about big Betty, eh?' Friend, you are on the spot. You have to explain who big Betty is *and* why you went purple. If you don't then the evening is ruined.

But in every humiliation there is a lesson to be learned – the bigger the humiliation the more important the lesson becomes. So I am going to tell you about one of my own personal disasters.

Situation

I was working for the Council Building Department as an apprentice plasterer. In those days we were building hundreds of council houses every year. The 'corpy' was a very steady place to work in. No bonus scheme, no scamping the job, and eleven hours' overtime every week (except in winter when it became dark early). Everyone was in the union – it was a condition of employment. But there were very few real trade unionists. The majority were just card-holders – and *how* they moaned.

'The union's nothing more than a licence to work!'

'It's a waste of time – we never see an official coming round the site.'

'What does the union do for us?'

To me, a lot of this talk was plain heresy. I'd been brought up in a home where it was expected that we would be 'active members' of the trade union. My Dad worked in an organized factory where the union (at that time) really carried some weight.

Now the postwar generation was quite different. Two of the liveliest young men were Tommy and Benny. They were in their middle twenties, both single, and they had completed two years' National Service in the Army. As everyone said, 'They just didn't give a monkey's!'

I worked with Tommy and Benny for six months. Never a day dragged. We'd be singing at the tops of our voices as we worked, or acting about. Working as a team we were fast, left a good job and had time to spare. So, for part of the day we'd hang out of the windows cracking jokes or shouting abuse at any of our mates coming. Do you know, people used to make a detour to get insulted by the three of us! I suppose it broke the day up for them and made life more interesting.

Neither Tommy nor Benny were much interested in overtime. They would *never* work a Saturday afternoon; they might during the week work the standard $1\frac{1}{2}$ hours' overtime *if it was raining*! Usually they would cycle off the site at 4.30 pm shouting at the older men, 'Slaves . . . slaves. No wonder your wife's gettin' a lodger!' Or else they would ask a tradesman, 'Now then Harry, who's the most time in this week – you or the lodgeman's cat?' Before getting an answer they'd ride away laughing.

The Sacking

Old Jacko, the foreman, was as crafty as they came. The way he sacked Tommy and Benny was an object lesson. He took me away from them and put me to work with sour-faced Harry. Then he sent Tommy and Benny patching up for the painters, with a labourer to help them. But there wasn't enough work patching to keep one apprentice busy – never mind three men. So both Tommy and Benny were miserable making the work spin out.

The foreman's next step was to take the labourer away. Neither of the tradesmen could protest in face of the obvious shortage of work. But having to labour on themselves was another humiliation. In fact, within a week they were completely demoralized. Tommy and Benny were clocking off at 4.30 even when it was raining. They went as far as taking three days' holiday to let the work build up before them after Jacko had suggested they look around for another job.

At that time there were over twenty plasterers working eleven hours' overtime a week. So when I went home one evening and told my Dad that Jacko had given Tommy and Benny their notice he was astounded.

'It's against all the principles of trade unionism,' he declared. 'No man should be sacked while overtime's being worked.'

'There's plenty of jobs in the town,' I told him, 'with better money. In fact, some of the tradesmen say that Tommy and Benny have been pampered. They say that in the 1930s they were sacked on the day they finished their apprenticeship.'

'Forget about the 1930s. What about the overtime?'

'Old Jacko says that it will be knocked off for a fortnight after they've been sacked,' I explained. 'Then we'll go back onto a 6 o'clock finish.'

My Dad was disgusted!

Militancy?

The next day I called on Benny and Tommy to see if they would put up a fight. Tommy said that he was pleased to be sacked. He was going to take his superannuation as a lump sum and buy a motorcycle. Benny was more annoyed, but his complaint was at being singled out.

'We're the fastest pair of plasterers on the site,' he complained. 'And he sacks us instead of some of those slow old 'uns. It's just victimization!'

'Let's go down to the branch meeting,' I suggested. 'Let's stir it up.'

Benny agreed but Tommy wouldn't join us.

'If we make trouble now,' he said, 'Jacko'll never have us back. Work might be scarce one day and being in Jacko's good books might make all the difference.'

By the time we had finished work that day my imagination was running riot. I was certain there would be a big debate and the branch would order the notices to be lifted. It would be the start of a new era of trade unionism in the Corporation. I fancied myself as the hero of the day.

Once we arrived at the branch meeting my fantasies crashed. There were only twelve members there, most of them old, all of them strangers. The Chairman nodded when we took our seats.

'I'll open the meeting now, he said, 'And I'm glad to see a couple of fresh faces here . . .'

Of course, I was wound up like a spring and frightened in case there was a hostile reception. At this gesture of friendliness I shot to my feet and gabbled, 'Yes, well you see Benny has been given his notice. And it's all wrong. It's against every principle of trade unionism . . .'

'Hang on. Hang on!' shouted the Chairman. 'Raise it later in the meeting. We have an agenda to follow, young fella. Now, Mr Secretary, could you please read the minutes of the last meeting?'

With the voice of doom the Secretary read through the minutes. There were some long-winded circulars from Head Office, a couple of letters, a report from the Trades Council Delegate and another from the area executive. It was all excruciatingly boring. I was miles away when suddenly the Chairman spoke to the meeting at large and me in particular.

'Anything under any other business?'

Benny nudged me.

I blurted out again, 'Oh . . . well . . . yes. You see, they're sacking Benny and Tommy next week. Tommy wouldn't come because he wants to buy a motorcycle. And my Dad says . . .'

It was a peculiar sensation. Something inside me was detached and listening to the story as I told it. The more I explained the less sense it made. I could feel my mouth drying. The words came out in a rush . . . I knew my face was a bright red. I wanted to get to the heart of the matter but I didn't know how to.

There was a good fifteen seconds' silence after I had finished. They were afraid I might start up again.

Then the Chairman asked, 'And what do you want this branch to do?'

'I don't know.'

The Chairman turned to Benny, 'You're the man who's being sacked. What's your story?'

'Oh, I'm not really bothered one way or another. Plenty of work around, isn't there?'

Then the card steward rose to his feet.

'I'm afraid, Mr Chairman, young Bob is trying to make a mountain out of a molehill. If you close the meeting I'll give you, privately, the *true* details of what the position is at the Corporation.'

To my astonishment the meeting was closed and the Chairman went into a huddle with the card steward and Benny. I sat there as though my feet were nailed to the floor.

The story that emerged was quite different from the one I'd told. There was a breeze-block shortage, so the bricklayers were building the shells of houses without completing the interior walls. There was a temporary shortage of work for plasterers. The Corporation didn't want to sack some of the older men because they were in bad health. Although the overtime was being suspended it would be reintroduced as soon as possible because of the shortage of council houses.

Jacko was giving Benny and Tommy their notice because they were the best of the young generation of plasterers. He thought they would benefit from working on top-class commercial jobs outside the Corporation. Jacko had advised them to leave their superannuation with the Corporation, and not to draw it out. He hoped that they would draw the obvious conclusion that they could return to their jobs once the crisis was over.

I felt completely destroyed. To make matters worse the card

steward said that I was a trouble-maker. 'Too bloody smart for his boots,' was another of his verdicts. Shaking his head, the Chairman observed that on that evening's performance he'd have said that I was as thick as two short planks!

It ended with the Chairman putting his arm round Benny's shoulders and telling him that he'd get him a job. I left, sick, sorry and vowing never to go to another branch meeting in my life. (Five years later I *was* the Chairman – another broken promise!)

Worse was still to come. When I told my Dad he laughed and said that I hadn't missed one mistake in the book. I went to bed muttering darkly about breaking my indentures and joining the Army.

Analysis

In retrospect I can see that I fell headlong into two major traps that lie in wait for the unwary. Even the most experienced politicians, community leaders and trade union leaders get caught in them. I call these traps 'freelancing' and 'phoney problems'.

Freelancing

Freelancing is the adoption of other people problems for one's own *personal* satisfaction while holding in contempt the established procedures for sorting out such problems. Some middle-class interference into working-class life falls into this category.

In most cases, workers, trade unions and management will not tolerate a freelance activist because he is only responsible to himself. An effective activist must be affiliated; he has to be responsible to other people.

Freelancing is, however, a constant temptation for most activists. But usually the ultimate result is someone being crucified, either the freelancer or the unfortunate person he adopts. Even so there are some highly skilled freelancers around in party politics, community politics and the trade unions. You can recognize them by their heavy air of integrity and responsibility, which is nothing more than a cloak. Once you hear the words 'Of course, you do realize that it has got nothing to do with me,' deep breath, '*but* . . . ,' start running.

Phoney Problems

Phoney problems are created when a *real* situation is interpreted in an *unreal* way by the people directly involved. Take Benny: he was irritated rather than injured. He wasn't even half behind the action we were taking, so it was nothing more than a phoney problem. Remember the rule: *phoney problems always evaporate when the heat comes on.*

Phoney problems are created by innocents or cynics. Innocents are so involved with their own reaction to a situation, like mine to Benny and Tommy's sacking, that they fail to see a phoney problem. One difficulty is that people have a tremendous capacity to accept and adjust to intolerable circumstances. They will agree with you that things are bad, and something should be done. But don't assume that this means that they will be a witness on their own behalf. In many cases they won't.

Cynics create and maintain a stock of phoney problems, and they are sometimes aided and abetted by their 'opposition'. Once phoney problems begin to appear in a negotiation, by some peculiar process people begin to lose sight of the real problems. There are benefits to the negotiators: with phoney problems they can afford to strike dramatic poses and concentrate on their style. Some trade unions, certain Whitehall pressure groups and all opposition political parties show a definite preference for phoney problems.

THINGS TO THINK ABOUT

1. How many freelancers are there in your situation?
2. Who or what controls freelancing and keeps it down to a minimum?
3. Are your *phoney problems* home-made or do you get them wholesale?

THINGS TO DO

1. Make a list of the different steps you would take if you were faced with a sacking.
2. Make a list of the preparations you would make before raising a formal complaint at a meeting.

Sequel

Plastering is hard work and the heaviest and most basic job is *floating*, that is, putting the first coat of plaster on the walls. It is all right for a short spell, but after a while it becomes tedious.

After the debacle at the branch meeting Old Jacko sent me floating, and for eighteen months I did nothing else. I was sick. Sometimes I'd shout to him, 'Eh Jacko . . . I've just broken Nelson's record for nonstop floating. How about a change?' But it didn't make any difference.

The other sequel was Jacko's warning that once I left the 'corpy' he would never take me back. Tommy and Benny returned to their jobs at the Corporation. But Jacko kept his promise after I left, and there was never an opening for me on the Corporation again. And I suspect that I am still on his blacklist to this day!

Section II And Another Thing . . .

Every activist scratches his head and asks himself at some time or another, 'Who the hell do *they* think I am?' There's another question, too, that strikes unexpectedly: 'What the hell am *I* doing this for?' If these questions haven't hit you yet – just wait, they're coming!

A psychologist using the jargon would call these questions *identity problems*. Knowing what to call them doesn't really provide the solutions. But this section is a start; it puts forward a number of ideas and techniques that you can use to *answer these questions for yourself.*

I assume that you are an activist. I assume that you want to develop your own *personality* and become more *effective*. I assume that as well as reading this book you are prepared to *work* to develop your ability. The work set out at the end of each chapter under the headings 'Things to Think About' and 'Things to Do' is designed for your maximum benefit. My advice is: *do not move on to another chapter until you have worked through this.* I want you to go back and answer the questions and complete the projects at the end of Chapter 1 before you read Chapter 2.

Finally, in the following chapters you may meet words that are new or unfamiliar. Don't skip over them. Note them down and check them in a dictionary. You never know, these words may be making a bottleneck in your mind.

---

2. Roles

Situation

Dai was a funny chap. When he was scrum-half he was always acting as if he were the captain of the team. When we made him captain he didn't want the job. 'I don't want to make a decision, I'm only one of the lads, *really*.'

Roles in plenty
when the class
war breaks out

It was the same when he was courting. Anyone would have taken him for a henpecked husband, 'Yes love, no love,' running round as though he was daft. But once he was married he immediately began acting as though he was single. Every night he was out boozing, and he was always prepared to stay up all night playing cards.

In the drawing office he'd tell the other draughtsmen, 'Don't get technical with me, boy, I'm only a simple fitter, *really*.' But when he visited the shop floor he came across as though he was next in line for the works manager's job!

Dai's behaviour did not match the different situations he was in. To use a technical term: Dai confused his *roles*.

Analysis

The notion of a *role* can be very useful. Having a role means that you are *sensitive* to certain situations and that you will behave in a *predictable* way when they occur. In Dai's case he was very sensitive to a situation but he enjoyed behaving in an unpredictable way. That is why everybody knew him and liked him. He was never another role in the crowd!

Do not confuse a *role* with *acting*; it goes much deeper than that. A role is tied up with our identity and our personality. Ask a person the vague question, 'Who are you?' and the chances are that a whole variety of *roles* will flash through his mind.

They might include:

Role	Situation
Father	With his children
Fan	At the match
Comedian	With his friends
Goalkeeper	With the works team
Boozer	Down the pub
Shop steward	With his workmates

Notice how each role relates to different groups of people. The technical term for this is the *reference group*.

Identity

The sum of a person's different roles do not completely answer the question, 'Who are you?' There is much more to a human being than that. He is the product of his experience, he is shaped and directed by his family, friends, the living and the dead. Roles exist in the present but personalities are rooted in the past and reflect our view of the future.

There is another reason why roles and personality are not identical. Many people use their formal roles as a shield to deflect criticism or to hide their true feelings. Policemen, quality control inspectors, bailiffs and foremen feel compelled to say, at one time or another, 'Don't blame me, I'm only following instructions.' Who hasn't used that excuse sometime?

The most important feature of the activist's role is that he has *chosen* it. No one can be forced to be an activist, although a reverse gravity seems to operate: it is always easier to pick up an activist's role than it is to drop it. An activist cannot hide behind his role because people say, 'If you don't believe in it, don't do it!' There is no convincing reply.

Activists and Other People

In any situation it is possible to identify six different kinds of people:

1. Professional – involved, expected to take initiatives, expected to control and serve the 'organization' (*role* and *job* combined).
2. Activist – involved and expected to take initiatives (*role* and *job* separate).
3. Playing member – involved when asked.
4. Non-playing member – inside but not involved.
5. Outsider – critical but not involved.
6. Spectator – not involved.

It is valuable to look at these, and at the behaviour associated with them, in greater detail.

1. *Professional*

The task of the professional is to bring continuity to the action and coordinate the activists. In this case the *role* and the *job* are combined. Because of this the professional will normally be less militant than the activist, *except* when his job is threatened. When that happens the professional will always prove that he is not a paper tiger, and his ferocity in such a situation can be quite unrestrained. However, one industrial disease affects most professionals: as they advance in years they tend to suffer from creeping complacency and delusions of invulnerability.

2. *Activist*

The task of the activist is to keep the action going. The activist's *role* is quite distinct from his *job*, which makes him an amateur in the true sense of the word: he does it for love. But he has to be prepared to take his own decisions, his own punishment and his own personal satisfaction in what he does. If he does not gain this satisfaction he can become a professional.

"'course.. they're all on an ego trip!"

Spectator   Outsider

Non-playing member

3. *Playing member*

The playing member will become involved in the action *provided he is asked.* But there are limits. If too much work is demanded of him the playing member will become a non-player. If he is pushed further he is likely to drop out of the organization altogether.

4. *Non-playing member*

The task of the non-playing member is to take the benefits; he provides the justification for the action. In some voluntary organizations he has to pay his dues, in which case he has the option of being a licensed critic as well. (It is the outsider who is the unlicensed critic.)

Playing member

Activist

Professional

5. *Outsider*

The outsider's task is to keep himself either indignant or fascinated. He works at it because he has to form his own attitudes and opinions. Outsiders should not be confused with professional critics who have a job, a role and an audience. Outsiders have none of these. The majority of them are lonely people, merely unlicensed critics trying to live through the experiences of other people (there are a thousand variations on the peeping-Tom act and only a few of them concerned with sex). Some outsiders hope that the mass media will notice them and publicize their complaints. This sometimes happens – but never on the outsider's terms. The mass media often use these people in order to add colour, 'human interest', or respectability to an otherwise dubious campaign.

Tolerance, dignity and humour are usually the best responses to outsiders. Most of them would prefer to be members or activists and with a modicum of skill they can often be brought inside the fold. (Ernest Bevin, one of the greatest British trade union leaders, was in his early years a rank outsider!)

6. *Spectator*

A spectator's main preoccupation is keeping himself amused. Because of this he concentrates on the excitement, the variety and the change in any situation. He is not as much interested in *understanding* a situation as in following the action. If there is little action then the spectator's attention will wander to something else. The large-circulation newspapers, the *Express*, the *Daily Mirror* and the *Sun* are written almost exclusively for spectators, for lively people with grasshopper minds. It is sobering to remember that on most issues the majority of the population is made up of spectators.

Analysis

Usually careful study is necessary to decide whether a person is an outsider or a member. Councillor Jones was a dedicated political activist who impressed everyone with his virulent attacks on organized religion. So there was general disbelief when he married his daughter off in the Church of England complete with all the nuptial trimmings. But when the Councillor was accused of being a hypocrite his reply was, 'I was baptized and went to Sunday school like everyone else . . . I'm a member.' The mistake was on our part. We had assumed that the Councillor was an outsider, an unlicensed critic, but he had his licence, though he kept it well hidden.

Very interesting, you may say, but what use *are* these six categories? In fact, they are a useful tool for analysing situations. Take the example of the management in a factory allowing the convenor of shop stewards an office and relieving him of his normal duties. Most shop stewards would be delighted at this 'victory'. But what they do not always realize is that in this way the convenor has been thrust from the ranks of the activists into the ranks of the professionals. Because of this the convenor will *inevitably* develop new perspectives and begin to behave differently. No one should be surprised – but everyone always is!

Here is another way in which the categorization can be used to analyse a situation: ask yourself how many of your so-called activist friends are in reality only playing members. This is often a crucial question. Most activists overestimate the amount of organized support they have in any situation. This is a matter of little consequence until there is a dispute. But when the crunch comes and the organization is 'hammered', the activist may be astounded to watch as many as 70 per cent of his colleagues disappearing into the ranks of the non-playing membership. Only then does he realize that as well as phoney problems there are also phoney activists.

In most situations the professional has a better idea of what the true strength of a situation is. Because of this professionals are sometimes wrongly accused of being pessimists, or of being unwilling to fight. *Professionals fight to win.*

THINGS TO THINK ABOUT

1. Are you really a playing member? (Remember an activist is not necessarily better than a playing member.)
2. Do you know what your role is? Does it blur round the edges?

THINGS TO DO

1. Write down four situations which would raise important issues for you. Indicate the different steps you would take in each of them.
2. On the basis of these four situations, work out in detail your *reference groups* and rate them in order of importance.

---

3. Relationships

Situation

Jock Brown was a regular in the local British Legion and everybody liked him. Not that he ever said much. He was a smiler, a nodder and a winker, who could tell you more with a tilt of his head and a lifting of an eyebrow than most people could with ten minutes' talk. Oh, and he never ducked a round.

Jock was a carpenter but his fame in the Legion came from his skill in organizing a flitting. He never refused to help a friend. Some of the jobs he tackled were unbelievable. One, with a grand piano, took three days, demolished a staircase, needed a breakdown truck and resulted in two ruptures. But everyone agreed that without Jock they'd have had to pull the house down. That story was told and retold for weeks – getting wilder with every retelling – with Jock visibly controlling a smile, nodding to himself and saying nothing.

Then someone did Jock a bad turn. He was nominated to become Pensions and Welfare Officer. It seemed a good idea at the time; after all, Jock was everybody's friend, always willing to help. It was an important job because people were constantly coming to the Legion for help with war and widows pensions. Sometimes, a neighbour would call in to say that an old soldier was having a struggle. There were new problems and fresh faces to deal with every week.

After four months the complaints started. Nothing could be

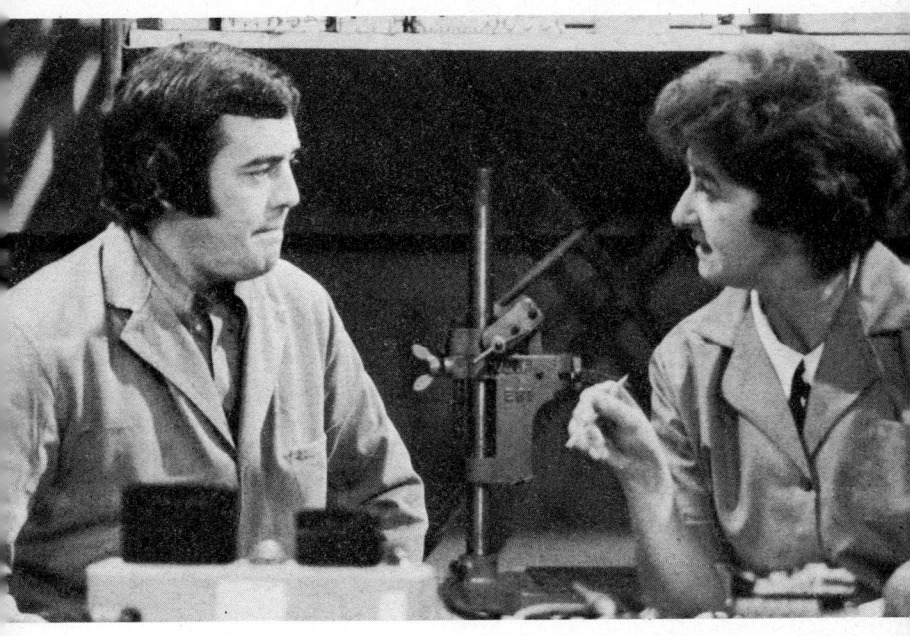

pinpointed, but some of the pensioners weren't happy with Jock. Within six months he had developed a nervous tic. His doctor told him to stop being an activist. Finally, Jock resigned from the club and started boozing at the Gas and Electric. The last I heard was that everyone in the Gas and Electric knew him and liked him – and he was helping on flittings again!

The story of Jock Brown can be found repeated in almost any voluntary organization in the country. The outcome is inevitable. And it comes as a surprise to everybody when a popular man fails in a job that has been thrust upon him.

Why does it happen? The short answer is that the person concerned cannot handle certain types of close relationships. Jock's may have been a minor tragedy. But his problems were those which every activist faces: how to conduct an interview, and how to understand the interpersonal processes involved.

Analysis

Let us look at Jock Brown's case in greater detail. He always sat in the Legion perched on a stool in the corner of the bar facing the door. Nothing ever escaped his notice. There were half a dozen middle-aged ladies who had their own table in the club: a couple of widows and others who had husbands who preferred to work regular night-shifts. (For obvious reasons they were called the 'easy six'.) If anyone was curious to know which of them was 'booked' he only needed to give Jock 'the wire' across the room. Within minutes, with the slightest of eye movements, lip-pursing, shoulder-shrugging and fist-clenching, Jock could convey what the score was.

All this was very public. Anyone in the room studying Jock, providing he knew who or what was being referred to, would get the message. The same thing happened if an argument was in progress at the bar. One look at Jock and it was possible to tell whether it was football, sex or politics, and whether sense or nonsense was being talked. So everyone used Jock as a point of reference which made him the most *public* man in the club. He never had a private conversation with anyone – not even the barman. He betrayed no secrets. Everyone knew exactly where Jock stood – or at least they *thought* they did, and Jock was very, very popular.

A psychologist studying Jock would say that he was a master of the art of *non-verbal communication*, sometimes called *body language*: he could deliver a clear and simple message without using words. At the same time, Jock was a very poor *verbal communicator*. Possibly his non-verbal ability was some form of compensation.

Body language does three things:

1. It can *replace* speech.
2. It can *support* speech.
3. It can show *attitudes and emotions*.

It is simple but loaded with meaning. But it has its drawbacks: it is vague and it lacks logic. Even so, most psychologists agree that it is constantly used to establish and develop personal relationships.

In many cases, we look for honesty and solidarity not in *what* is being said but in the *way* it is being said. We give off non-verbal messages about friendship, hostility, boredom, interest and excitement without being aware of it. Yet these same messages are received and understood by our family and friends without *them* really being aware of it.

Body language might tell us how we stand in relation to another person very effectively. But there are real limits to the way it can be used. First, most people, apart from actors, use it instinctively rather than deliberately. Secondly, it is a very poor way of conveying a lot of information. Thirdly, it is limited usually to the here and now. Finally, it cannot deal adequately with *cause* and *effect*. All these limitations do not apply to verbal and written communication. Let us examine verbal skills a little closer. (Writing skills are dealt with later in this book.)

Jock Brown was severely handicapped because he could not conduct an effective interview. He found himself continually taking up the trivialities of a complaint rather than the substance. He accepted stories on their face value, and never tested their logic or consistency. He sympathized with everybody. He was incapable of digging beneath the surface in order to get at the root of a problem. So Jock became depressed and resigned from the job.

The fault wasn't Jock's. He should never have been forced into becoming an activist. His best role was that of a strong dependable *playing member*. It is doubtful if any training programme would have compensated for his weakness in verbal and written communication. But Jock was exceptional – a genius in one area and an idiot in another. This is not true of most people. Activists *can* become more effective in their relationships, *particularly in interviews*, providing that firstly they become more sensitive; secondly, they are able to put themselves in a member's shoes; and thirdly, they remember the simple rules of interviewing.

Interviews

Interviews are *purposeful encounters* with other people. They are *purposeful* because at least one of the people involved wants to obtain information out of the situation. They are *encounters* because normally they have a beginning and an end. A casual chat in a pub isn't an interview because it isn't purposeful. Husbands rarely 'interview' their wives because the relationship between them is permanent, that is, it is 'ongoing' and not subject to starts and stops, although it is often purposeful.

Social Sensitivity

The *meaning* of an interview will depend on a number of different factors: the listener, the speaker, their experience and command of language, their knowledge of one another and the *whole context* of the situation. If a person stops talking he does not stop communicating. His silence, his expression and the whole posture of his body may be expressive. Being sensitive means having an awareness of all these minute cues and clues and learning to read them correctly.

The context is all-important. If a policeman rushes into a theatre and yells 'Fire!' no one gives a damn about his heavy breathing.

It is impossible to develop social sensitivity if one's experience is confined to short brutal encounters with other people. The loud-mouth and the bully put themselves into a prison of low communication. People avoid them or keep contact for the minimum possible time.

There are psychologists who specialize in running training groups (sometimes called 'T-groups') and claim that they increase people's sensitivity. However, there are reasons for being suspicious of these claims. While the group sessions might be valuable to tough-minded professionals, I feel that they can be highly dangerous for activists. Too much 'sensitivity' can result in timidity, nervousness and too great an awareness of personal faults. My advice would be to stay away from 'T-groups', particularly if they are organized by professionals, because the result might be the increase of the powers of manipulation of the professionals and the weakening of the activist. Some managers believe that this can be justified if the 'organization is strengthened and becomes more humane'. I have my doubts. If you want to develop your social sensitivity it is better to do it yourself.

You can start by:

1. *Deliberately talking less and listening more.* This is one of the hardest things in the world to do; but it is the beginning of social control and development.

2. *Observing and trying to interpret other people's emotions and attitudes.* This is something that you already do instinctively. 'What are you looking so happy about?' you ask your friends. But deliberate and constant observation is necessary with a variety of different people if your powers are to be developed fully.

3. *Assessing other people's ability to express themselves in words.* A member may be able to *convey* his meaning, like Jock, without necessarily using words. He may expect his activist to help him in choosing the right words to fit the situation. This becomes crucial when a complaint is being dealt with. If the activist doesn't get the exact meaning he could find himself in trouble.

In fact, the only way to make an assessment of a person's verbal ability is to get him or her to talk. This means being a good listener.

The ability to put yourself in someone else's position is called empathy. Empathy is what you *feel* (sympathy is what you *give* to another person). A good interview requires both empathy and sympathy.

Take the example of a worker coming to see his shop steward with a minor problem. Let us try to see the interview through the worker's eyes. There are several hurdles to be taken.

1. *First Hurdle: Am I Welcome?* The worker doesn't know how he will be received. For this reason he will be casual and vague in his initial approaches. If the shop steward doesn't respond in an enthusiastic manner the worker may drift away.

2. *Second Hurdle: Am I Wasting Your Time?* The worker needs to tell his story but he is worried in case the shop steward will dismiss it as trivial. If he does so, then the worker's pride suffers. Therefore he may play the problem down until the shop steward agrees that it is important, or he may exaggerate the problem and the injury. However, once there is agreement that a problem exists, the interview can become more formal and more specific.

3. *Third Hurdle: Does He Think I Am Lying?* Once the problem has been identified it is necessary to establish its causes. The worker has then to re-examine his story so that it becomes a closer match to reality. The shop steward who says, 'But five

minutes ago you told me . . .' can interfere with this vital process.

4. *Fourth Hurdle: What Are We Going To Do?* Will the row over the problem cost too much? The worker worries in case he becomes a pawn in someone else's game. It is not uncommon for a worker to break off an interview at this hurdle. It may be he has got what he was after: the shop steward has agreed that a 'diabolical liberty' has been taken, and a coherent story has been made out of the problem which can be re-told to his family and friends. A good story that lasts a fortnight might be preferred to a problem that lasts one hour!

Remember that the four hurdles don't come up in any definite order. They are all present from the beginning of the interview and each has to be overcome if the interview is to be successful.

Empathy should be a two-way process. Also, members should be given some idea of what the activist wants from them. Usually it boils down to three things:

1. *Mutual respect.* No activist wants to be treated as a tool of the membership.
2. *Solidarity.* No activist wants to work for anyone who will repudiate his social obligations to his fellow-members.
3. *Truthfulness.* A member who tells lies is a walking booby-trap to the unwary activist. Once an activist believes a liar his own credibility can be destroyed.

I suggest that every activist should insist, quietly but firmly, on mutual respect, solidarity and truthfulness from his members. If these are not granted it is simpler and wiser to turn in one's credentials rather than wait to be destroyed by the opposition

Rules for Interviewers

Plan

Before an interview work out the kind of information you are seeking and how you propose to get it. (With an unexpected interview be prepared to take it in two stages. If necessary break off in order to plan and prepare.)

Control

The interviewer controls the *formality* or *informality* of the interview. Usually it is wise to start the interview as informally as posssible in order to put the member at ease. An informal approach often reveals the general background of the problem. However, a more formal approach often produces precise information and makes each person aware of the role that the other person is playing.

WEIGHING UP, WORKING OUT, HUNCHES

Being an activist involves tackling problems, weighing up a situation and taking decisions. So you have to:
1. Think things out.
2. Make choices.

Some choices are made on logical grounds, in other words, on the obvious implications of your thoughts. But others are made on an emotional and intuitive basis: you may not be able to explain the reasons for your choice either to yourself or someone else, but you feel it is right.

It is a mistake to think that logic and emotions can be separated. *Emotions always precede reason.*

It makes sense to get all the relevant facts about a problem or a situation. It is right to *weigh up* the facts and discard the irrelevant. You should *work out* the reasons, the causes and effects of problems. But, when you have worked through the problem you should still back your *hunch* if it is strong enough.

Never be frightened of emotions: they are an activist's biggest asset.

Questions

Usually the interview is controlled by using different kinds of questions. Beware of general questions which often produce confused and confusing answers and also make the member work harder in the interview than is necessary. Silence on your part is often the most effective question of all, since it can produce the kind of valuable and revealing information that intensive cross-questioning would bury.

Confidentiality

A relationship can be judged by the amount of confidential information that can be shared. It is a measure of the trust between the two parties. But *never* use confidential information in subsequent negotiations.

Taking Notes

Do not start taking notes until the full story has emerged. Decide yourself whether notes are necessary and *ask the member whether he agrees*. Be sure to check your notes with the member before the interview ends.

Review

After an important interview review the information obtained *before* taking action. Ask yourself:

1. Have I drawn all the information possible out of the interview?
2. Do I need more information and, if so, from what source?
3. Does the story need collaboration?

---

4. Social Power

Introduction

Over the past fifteen years I have listened to professors, politicians, union officials, councillors and shop stewards talking about power. In nine cases out of ten they have talked utter rubbish! I have often wondered why this should be. Perhaps it is because *power* is a dirty word in the twentieth century. Certainly, it is easier to ask someone about their sex life than about the amount of power they have and how they use it.

I have noticed that many people connect power with Attila the Hun, Stalin, Frankenstein, or Hitler. It is almost as if power were synonymous with ruthlessness and evil. These vivid images are a barrier to clear thinking. None of us are likely to meet Attila, Stalin, Frankenstein, or Hitler, so our wild notions about power are never challenged. In fact, while power is confused with hatefulness the truth remains that the most powerful person we are ever likely to meet is one of our parents. To know

what power is really about, think of your mother or your father. Their power may be small today – but at one time it was tremendous!

Definition

Social power is the ability to affect another person's behaviour. If you cannot produce some kind of change in what someone is going to do then you are powerless! Nothing could be more simple and obvious when you think about it. The bigger the change in behaviour the more power is involved.

Try to think of power as if it has two dimensions. The first dimension is an actual *exchange* between the parties involved; the exchange may involve money, affection, anger, violence, goods or good turns. In the second dimension there are *images* that exist between the parties; these may include the images of authority, solidarity, justice, or even motherhood. By examining these two dimensions in detail it is possible to create a useful *tool* to analyse power.

Analysis

The two dimensions of power have the different features as outlined.

Exchange Factors

Some social scientists suggest that there are two sides to the exchange dimension of social power: penalty factors and reward factors.

Research shows that using *penalties* (in other words, punishment) to change people's behaviour is inefficient (not to mention immoral). Also, the changes that do occur tend to be temporary. Once the penalties are withdrawn, behaviour usually reverts to its previous pattern, but the bitterness lingers on. Penalties also tend to be costly. Human ingenuity being what it is, penalties can be and are avoided. Through time, penalties can lose their sting and become accepted as normal liabilities.

With children it seems clear that penalties may rebound on the parent. As one study concluded:

'Mothers who punished toilet accidents ended up with bed-wetting children. Mothers who punished dependency to get rid of it had more dependent children than mothers who did not punish. Mothers who punished aggressive behaviour severely had more aggressive children than mothers who punished lightly.'*

Systematic *rewards* are a very effective way of changing a person's behaviour. Children whose achievements are rewarded by affection tend to work harder than those who aren't rewarded.

Life in a modern commercial society often turns on a system of rewards. If an employer wants someone to work longer hours he offers *overtime* rates. A father asking a child to run for an evening paper will say, 'Keep the change.'

There are scores of common phrases which express this side of social power. 'You scratch my back and I'll scratch yours.' 'Every man has his price.' 'If you ever do 'owt for nowt, do it for yourself.' 'Dog doesn't eat dog.'

If you are still doubtful about rewards, imagine that you have a boutique and want your supplier to change his line, adopt a new fashion or a new colour. Which argument do you think would persuade him of these two: 'If you don't change I'll try to put you out of business,' or 'If you do change I will increase my order by 50 per cent'? The first argument would surely provoke conflict, whereas the second might secure cooperation.

Image Factors

A lot of our knowledge about the world, and about people, is stored in the form of images which continuously modify our behaviour. Image power and exchange power are not separate things. You might *exchange* insults with someone you consider to be an absolute swine – and your *image* of him will be strengthened. On the other hand, it might have been the *image* that caused you to start exchanging insults in the first place. Images are the result of experience, learning and all forms of communication. They can be thought of as a *processed* stock of information. They are constantly being amended, revised, adopted or discarded.

* Robert R. Sears, Eleanor Maccoby, Harriet Leven, *Patterns of Child Rearing* (Harper & Row, New York, 1957), p. 484.

This analysis will concentrate on three factors involved in the image aspect of social power: identity, legitimacy, competence.

Identity elements   If we identify strongly with another person we have, in effect, licensed him to modify our behaviour if he wishes to. The young boy who strongly identifies with his father rarely poses a problem of discipline. However, once the son starts to search for his own identity a father's influence will decline. Some fathers take it badly.

The workers who identify with their shop steward, or convenor, will always accept their leadership much more willingly than workers who lack this identification.

Legitimacy elements   In some situations we change our behaviour because we feel that a legitimate request has been made. Consider a passer-by to whom a policeman says, 'I wouldn't go down that street if I were you.' Most people would pay attention to the policeman because his request, all other things being equal, is more likely to be legitimate.

The same would be true in an industrial dispute. 'The shop stewards' committee advises members to go slow.' This statement would be considered more legitimate, by the members, than one taken by a meeting of twenty-three casual passengers on a no. 14 bus.

Competence elements   It is difficult to ignore the advice of a competent person. You might have decided to buy a car, found the right model, colour and year. But if an A.A. or R.A.C. inspector declares it a liability at the price, only an insensitive or stupid person will complete the purchase. However, often competence isn't enough. Millions of smokers choose to ignore the advice of the most competent medical authorities that smoking damages their health.

Examples

We now have a *model* of social power that can be used to analyse different situations.

Remember that social power involves:

1. The *exchange* of *rewards* and *penalties*.
2. The *images* of *identity*, *legitimacy* and *competence*.

Example 1

Phil is a toolmaker and convenor in a car factory. How much power does he have over his fellow shop stewards?

Exchange   Phil's *rewards* and *penalties* are mostly verbal: he can either praise or blame. Some of the shop stewards will accept neither. He can threaten to have a steward's credentials withdrawn; this threat only carries weight with members of his own union. Conclusion: Phil has very little exchange power.

Image   Only the engineering shop stewards *identify* strongly with Phil. All the shop stewards consider his role to be *legitimate* because they gave him the power in the first place. But as Phil comes round for election every year his authority is questioned. The stewards agree that Phil is the most *competent* person for the job. But every couple of years, because of his identification weakness, the semi-skilled stewards replace him with one of their number. Invariably, after a year fraught with problems caused by incompetence. Phil is re-elected as convenor. Conclusion: Phil has considerable image power but it waxes and wanes over a period.

Example 2

Sam is a foreman in a small engineering works; like Phil he had served his time on toolmaking. How much power does he have over his workers?

Exchange   Sam can praise and blame his workers who usually have to accept it. He has substantial *rewards* to give: overtime, slack times for jobs, long tea-breaks. He can recommend workers for promotion. Each of these rewards, if reversed, can become a *penalty*. In addition, Sam has the added penalties of suspension and sacking *partly* in his grasp.

Image   Few of the workers *identify* with Sam, because he has 'gone over to the other side'. A large proportion of the workers feel that the shop would run quite effectively without him, so they question the *legitimacy* of his position. Likewise, Sam's *competence* is questioned. His fellow workers remember that he wasn't the best toolmaker in the shop, and that he was always crawling up to management. Conclusion: Sam has substantial exchange power but very little image power. Heaven help him if he has to go back on the shop floor again.

Warning! These two examples are only a means of exploring the ideas connected with social power. In practice it will be found that the *context* of a situation, that is, why, where and when it is happening, is often crucial. This chapter is to some extent an exercise in abstract thinking. And like all abstract ideas it should be put into practice *very carefully*. But once an activist begins to understand the mechanisms of social power he will be able to analyse the complexities of his role. He will begin to examine his personal strengths and his weaknesses and begin to see them as the key to effective action.

THINGS TO DO

1. Assess your strongest and weakest social power element.
2. Do the same for one of your colleagues.
3. Compare the two assessments. Are the differences significant
   – and why?

5. Social Groups

Introduction

Cattle live in herds, wolves live in packs, birds live in flocks, and men and women live in social groups. From birth we are claimed and raised by many different groups: our family, friends, relatives, neighbours, classmates, playmates, workmates, trade union colleagues and political associates. We are each part of overlapping circles of people, each circle in a way unique, each with a different set of *relationships* and requiring us to play a different *role*.

An activist needs to understand the nature of social groups. He needs to appreciate the pressure that a group can exert on people within it. Finally, he needs to be aware of the subtle changes that can and do take place between a group and its leadership.

Research

Over the past forty years there has been considerable research into social groups. One of the earliest experiments involved people watching a light in a darkened room. After a while the light appeared to move although, in fact, it was in a permanent fixed position. Everyone taking part in the experiment was asked to join a group to estimate the distance and direction that it was thought the light had moved. It was found that people's judgement converged on a *common group norm*. After the group had been dispersed this common norm was remembered and supported by the members. The same experiment discovered that the majority of people claimed that they had not been influenced by the other members of the group. It seems that we can be *affected* and yet remain *unaware* of group pressures.

* Research shows that under group pressure a minority of people will conform to judgements they know to be wrong!
* Group solidarity tends to be greatest when the problem is insoluble!

Groups, Organizations and Institutions

I was once talking to a group of trade union branch secretaries about social groups. Someone asked me whether the term covered a darts team in the local as well as a trade union. The answer was 'Yes'. But there are special terms which are used to distinguish between different kinds of social groups.

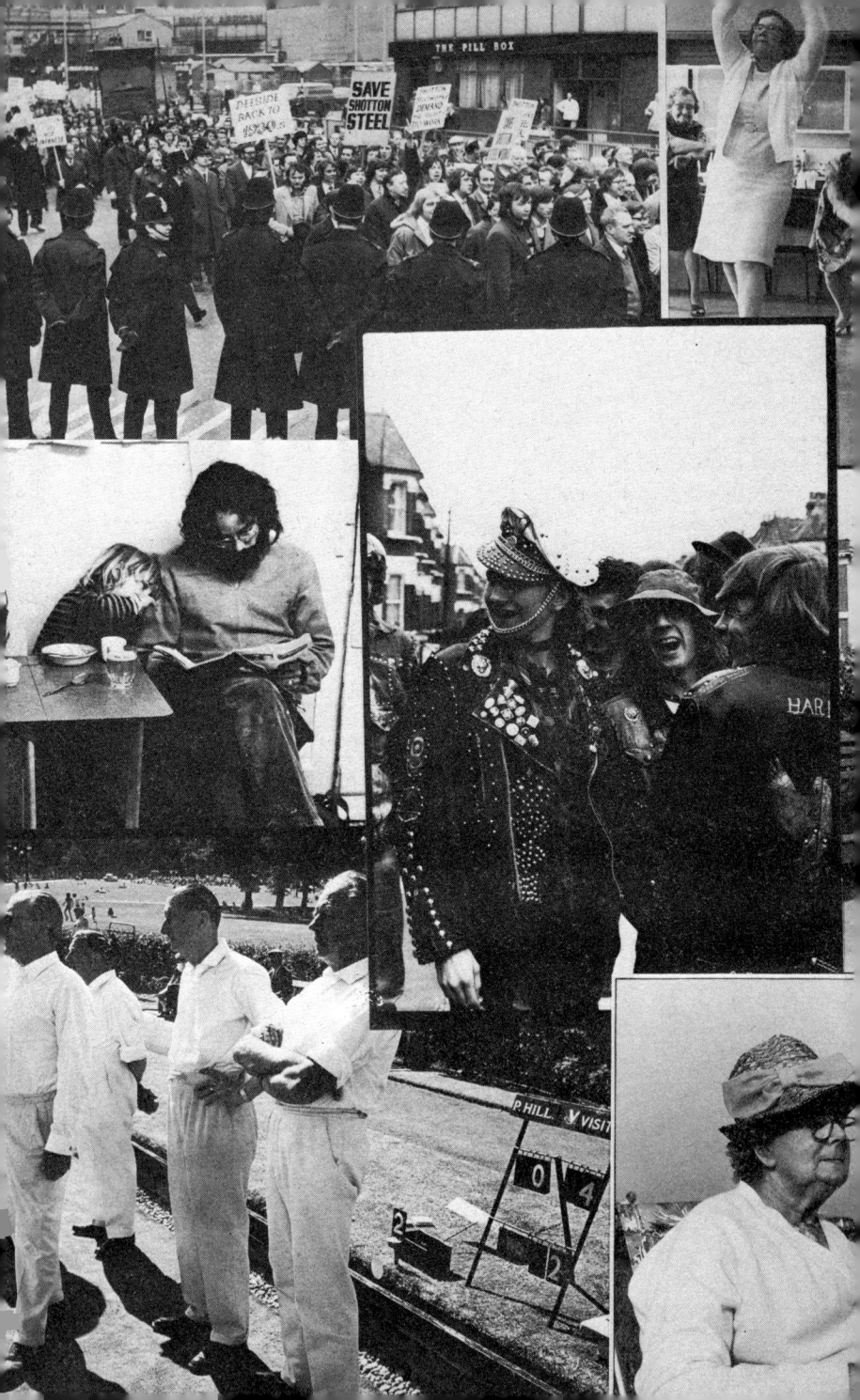

Informal Groups

These are made up of like-minded people who either take pleasure in each other's company or have similar goals. There are no *explicit* rules, policies, or goals involved and there are no visible forms of compulsion on the members. Equality is accepted.

Examples:

1. A casual darts match in a pub.
2. A group of workers chatting on the shop floor.

Formal Groups

These can be recognized by their obvious goals, procedures and rules. Within this group there are specialist roles which have to be carried out by designated members. Apart from these roles there is a degree of equality among the members.

Examples:

1. A match between two pub darts teams.
2. A group of workers talking about conditions of work, either on the shop floor or in a union branch.

Organizations

An organization can be defined as a formal group of formal groups. The goals and rules for an organization have to be more explicit and obvious. It *controls* the formal groups within it. An organization is usually based on a pyramid of authority and power, and equality may not exist between the different levels. This is sometimes called the *hierarchy* of the organization.

Examples:

1. The organization and fixture list of all a town's pub darts teams.
2. A trade union.

Institutions

These are organizations with a *name*, an *identity* and a recognized *role* in relation to the rest of society. The difference between 'organization' and 'institution' is usually one of perspective: in the first we look at the *inside*, and in the second we look at the *outside*, of the same thing. To examine the *organization* of the Engineering Union it would be necessary to look at the constitution and the way power and authority is divided between the branches, district committees, the executive and the final appeal court. To examine the *institution* it would be necessary to look at the way apprenticeships are controlled, the way the union bargains about wages and working conditions, and its impact on industry and society.

Examples:

1. The National Darts Federation.
2. The Amalgamated Union of Engineering Workers: Engineering Section.

Remember that behind all social groups stand organizations and institutions both small and large, weak and powerful.

Groups and Leadership

Most activists find a great deal of overlapping between informal and formal groups. Before a shop steward is elected (that is, given a formal role) many of his workmates will have decided on the basis of their experience that he is acceptable and has leadership potential, that is, that he has been tested by informal groups. Most shop stewards are aware that there are informal leaders within the ranks of their members who may criticize and undermine the work that they do. Often formal and informal groups share the same personnel and have the same problems and preoccupations. However, the relationship between both kinds of social groups and their leaders has been studied in depth and a fairly definite, if composite, picture has emerged.

Profile of an Informal Group Leader

Imagine a group of friends who all support the same football team. One of them will have more influence than the others: he is the *opinion leader*. This person will be better informed about the team and football generally than the others. He will have the same attitudes to the team but he will hold them more strongly and express them more often. It is also likely that he will go to more matches, read more newspaper reports and know more supporters than the rest of the group.

If the team suddenly signs a new striker from a Third Division Club the group as a whole will be undecided whether it is a good or a bad move. Should they applaud or condemn? The chances are that the opinion leader will make the final decision; if he approves the transfer everyone else will agree with him. However, if the transferred player proves to be a walking disaster the leader must change his opinion with the rest of the group, otherwise his credibility will be destroyed and the group will look for another opinion leader.

You can see that there is a delicate balance between the group and its leader. They are both interdependent. In some cases the group can force someone to become the opinion leader by continually asking questions on a given topic. After a while the person concerned will become *sensitive* to that topic and begin gathering and remembering information about it. A role will have been *thrust* on him.

In one of the Merseyside car factories there was an ardent Everton supporter, Rolly Brennan. As a joke all his workmates pretended he was a Liverpool supporter. They never asked him about Everton and pestered him with questions about the Anfield team. Within the space of one month they made him an expert. After three months Rolly began watching Liverpool when Everton was away, something his brother, who worked in the same factory, had bet £10 that he would never do. Of course, it was the man who organized the 'joke' who collected the £10. Shrewd!

Groups and Solidarity

Solidarity is one of the key issues within a group. Without solidarity the group will cease to exist and the members will be 'poorer' as a result. It is possible to specify those factors which make for high solidarity.

1. *Similarity*. The more things a group of people have in common the greater the solidarity. There are some unpalatable conclusions to be drawn from this. *If everything else is equal*

there will be greater solidarity within single sex or single race groups than mixed groups.

2. *Pressures for conformity.* The more willing a group is to exclude or punish a member the stronger become the bonds that keep them together. This means that the more intolerant a group is, the greater its power.

3. *Equality.* The greater the equality between members the greater the solidarity. This means that a social group can be weakened if someone deliberately sets out to make the members unequal. Management, politicians and youth club leaders have discovered through experience that a few well-chosen awards, gifts and medals can help to neutralize informal opposition.

4. *Participation.* The opinion leader who makes judgements without consulting his group helps to destroy its solidarity. Without participation social groups will wither and die. With greater participation solidarity increases.

5. *Issue.* The bigger an issue is seen to be, the greater is the solidarity induced. This is where the opinion leader's role is often crucial. If he learns to build up the significance of issues he can create a tremendous sense of solidarity. However, if this technique is constantly used and taken to extremes it produces a fundamental conservatism within the group, which becomes paranoid about outsiders and fearful of any change. Then solidarity becomes a trap from which it is difficult to escape.

6. *Membership changes.* No social group can survive large and frequent changes in membership and continue to be effective. Sometimes when informal groups within factories develop high solidarity, this creates resentment all round. A sophisticated manager faced with this problem might identify the opinion leader and either promote him or wait until he is absent before dispersing the group. In other cases, particularly with women workers, the membership is deliberately maintained for years by management because of high morale and high productivity within the group.

7. *Dependence.* The more the members of a group depend upon each other the greater the solidarity will be. In such circumstances a threat to one becomes a threat to all.

8. *Interaction*. The more often the members of a group interact with each other – meet, chat, signal and share – the higher their solidarity is likely to be. Every interaction is an opportunity for communication between people, an opportunity to develop common attitudes and common responses to situations.

Through understanding these factors it is possible to make a rough prediction about the solidarity among different groups of people. For instance, take a group of men and women cleaners in a factory; they are easy-going, some are highly paid, others low. The shop steward never consults them; they are never faced with a big issue; their labour turnover is high; they are not dependent on each other, and rarely meet. It is *predictable* that this group will be apathetic and lacking in solidarity. On the other hand, take a group of toolmakers, all men. They won't tolerate even a fitter working with them; they are all on the same rate of pay; they make decisions together; they are constantly faced with attacks on their craft and status; their membership rarely changes; they are highly interdependent, and continually talk among themselves. It is *predictable* that this group will have conservative attitudes compared with other workers and will be a powerful force within the factory.

Formal and Informal Group Leaders

We are now in a position to examine the differences between formal and informal group leaders. Let us look at the relationship between the group and the leader in terms of *social power*. The informal group leader owes his position mainly to image power: the rest of the group *identifies* with him and recognizes his *competence*. The question of legitimacy does not arise as far as the group is concerned. With the formal group leader identification and competence are important, but so is the *legitimacy* of his role. This is not decided by the group, but by the organization of which the group is a part. For example, a shop steward is elected by his workmates, and also his role is made legitimate by the granting of credentials by the trade union.

* For formal group leaders the legitimacy of their role is crucial.
* For informal group leaders the legitimacy of their role is irrelevant.

* In a formal group people know when they are leaders.
* In an informal group people are never certain what their role status really is at any point in time.

THINGS TO THINK ABOUT

1. Do you think that it is inevitable that every organization has a hierarchy? Is it desirable?
2. Why do people claim that other members of a group have had no influence on them?
3. Do you face any insoluble problems at present? What is your attitude to them?

THINGS TO DO

1. Make a list of the important formal groups you belong to.
2. Try to identify the informal groups that overlap those formal groups and assess their importance.
3. To what extent do your formal groups attempt to ignore the organizations of which they are a part? Make a list of the ways the organizations are ignored.

Section III Working the System

Most working-class activists are happiest when they are in an informal group. Instinctively, they distrust formal organizations because of the emphasis on procedure, and because of the different levels of authority (which the smokescreen of pledges of equality cannot really hide). Often this distrust is a valuable protection for the activist, because it prevents him from becoming gullible, and stops the organization from becoming too manipulative.

It *is* important to know what organizations are about and how they operate. They are part of the world we were born into. As a plasterer I benefited from the struggles of a Victorian generation of craftsmen who founded the union. They created an organization I was proud to join almost a hundred years later: a union which gave me rights and protected my interests.

The Victorian workers learned a basic lesson the hard way. They found out that informal social groups can be destroyed easily by the superior power of the employers. A formal organization, the union, was essential for their own dignity, protection and survival. And the men who created the union were worried about power. They didn't want it concentrated in a few hands. So they wrote a constitution that attempted to keep the maximum amount of power in the hands of the members. That constitution remained the heart of the union. Together with the Rule Book it was the essential contract between the members, the executive and the full-time officials.

The constitution of most voluntary organizations is similar to the wiring diagram of a car. If you understand it, and follow it through, you can see how one centre of power connects with another. If you know where the key 'switches' are, you can 'turn on' the organization and make it perform. The 'switches' to be learned are *committees*, *delegates*, *conferences*, *resolutions*, *reports*, *speeches* and *letters*. These are the things that will be dealt with in this section.

I don't want to lull you into a false sense of security. I don't necessarily want you to become less critical of the organizations of which you are a part. Understanding how hierarchies operate in organizations should not be the same as saying they are 'right', 'normal', or justified in every situation. The activist should be aware that knowing the rules and using the rules are the first steps in a conditioning process. This knowledge and skill becomes a source of power in itself. So be careful!

---

6. Organizations

Introduction

Many of the key voluntary organizations in this country were created by our grandfathers and great-grandfathers. Some are so familiar that today we treat them with indifference. But these organizations offer many opportunities to an activist who understands the way they operate and who is prepared to use them *creatively*. And imagination, energy and persistence are essential.

Why bother? Well, organizations can compensate for the vulnerability and weakness of the individual activists. They can outlive individuals. They are storehouses of social power. By specializing and concentrating money, time and energy they can tackle problems which overwhelm a single person. Without organizations many activists would be merely latter-day Don Quixotes, tilting at windmills and freelancing their way through life.

Definition

We have already defined an *organization* in a previous chapter by contrasting it with informal social groups. However, it is useful to have an even more precise definition.

An organization is a permanent communication system made up of formal groups of people with explicit goals, roles, procedures and rules.

Let us look at each part of this definition in turn.

Permanence: renewal and survival If human beings cannot take in new energy in the form of food they eventually die. The same is true of an organization. But where the body needs food, an organization needs people. Men and women are elected or removed from formal roles as the situation changes. By controlling this 'ebb and flow' into and out of office, the organization usually manages to renew itself.

Renewal is concerned with relationships inside the organization; survival depends on the relationship with society. Sometimes society or the state becomes hostile. For example, Hitler destroyed trade unions when he came to power. The 1800 Combination Act in England was an attempt to prevent workers forming trade unions. But even in favourable environments organizations have to struggle to survive and sometimes suppress their goals and their principles in order to do so (see below).

The communication system An organization depends on an internal circulation of information which is as vital as the blood in a human body. A voluntary organization, in particular, needs a vigorous two-way flow of information. Secrecy, once it creeps in, starts a rotting process which destroys solidarity, denies equality and undermines democracy. Membership of a voluntary organization confers a basic right to information, a right which no one is entitled to deny.

Goals, roles, procedures and rules The goals of a voluntary organization are clearly visible. The members know what they want. But, as Bernard Shaw pointed out, there are two tragedies in life: one is wanting something badly and not getting it; the other is wanting something badly and getting it.

These tragedies happen with an organization. First, if it doesn't reach the desired goal, how can it survive? One method is to strengthen the internal rules and procedures so that critics within the ranks are purged and forced to become outsiders. Another tactic is to launch a campaign in order to create a religious mentality in the membership. In this way fervour is substituted for practical achievements. The image of the promised land, although deferred, is made even more mystical.

The goals, roles, procedures and rules of an organization are usually adjusted *together* to cope with any new situation. It is this *interconnection* which the effective activist should always look for, and be aware that it usually takes a balance of *exchange* and *image* power to keep an organization together.

What happens when the goal is attained? Does the organization go out of business? Research says 'No'. In fact, there i˙ a famous law, Robert Michels' 'iron law of oligarchy',* which maintains that the survival of the organization ultimately and inevitably becomes the major goal. This goal *displaces* all others in importanre. And if the *original* goal of an organization is achieved the professionals usually replace it with something else.

Trade Unions and Social Power: Some Notes

The framework we developed in Chapter 4 can be used to analyse an organization. As an illustration, the power relationship between a trade union and its members will be examined.

It has already been pointed out that trade unions are storehouses of social power. They store both exchange and image factors which influence their members' behaviour. Before we start the analysis, however, it is useful to look at the common observation that a trade union is the members. This is true. But it is like saying that the Mona Lisa is a square of wood with pigment-daubed canvas. By being a *partial* statement it misleads by ignoring the heart of the matter. The *full* statement should be as follows.

A trade union is the members acting collectively to achieve common goals, operating within a constitution and guided by a Rule Book.

Exchange Factors

Rewards   If we look back to the Victorian period we find that the craft unions offered their members substantial rewards in the form of friendly society benefits. If a member was ill or unemployed the union would pay him benefits. If he died it would

* Robert Michels, *Political Parties* (Dover, New York, 1959).

help bury him. However, these direct rewards have become much less important under the welfare state.

In the United States, where the social services are more primitive, many trade unions still provide substantial friendly society benefits and medical and dental services.

The major rewards British unions can offer their members today are first, representation, and second, protection. In the case of a pre-entry closed shop there is an additional reward of access to jobs.

Penalties   Despite the statements of politicians and the stories of the popular press, most trade unions have little punitive power. Generally, trade unions are not feared as much as either managers who can sack, suspend and demote workers, or informal work-groups who can send people to Coventry. Of course, there are disciplinary rules in the union Rule Books, but penalties should be definite, obvious and inevitable in order to be effective. However, as operated by unions they are usually vague, unknown, uncertain and hedged around with appeals procedures.

Unions do have more influence over professionals and activists. By withdrawing credentials and stripping people of their formal roles a union declares that a man or woman is unfit to represent his fellow members. Many activists would consider this to be a terrible humiliation.

Image Factors

Identification   We would expect non-playing members to have a weak identification with a union, whereas professionals would have a strong identification. The activists and playing members would fall somewhere in between.

Is identification greater in craft unions than in general unions? This was so seventy years ago. Is it true today?

Members may confuse the identity of the institution with the leading official. This is a common tendency. Thus sometimes one hears activists talk about 'Hugh Scanlon's Engineering Union' and 'Jack Jones' Transport and General'.

Competence   A key issue for a trade union is the ease with which it can adjust to changing situations and changing goals. Perhaps the pattern of influence is the reverse of that suggested for identification. Professionals can often see evidence of incompetence from their vantage point within the organization. They can, and do, quote chapter and verse of union shortcomings among themselves. But non-playing members can remain in complete ignorance of these defects and are usually happy to assume that the union is competent because it *does* operate.

Legitimacy   The 1971 Industrial Relations Act attempted to impose its own definition of legitimacy on the trade unions. It failed because British unions have never looked outside their organization to justify their existence. Their main source of legitimacy has always been internal: the existence and availability of democratic decision-making within an agreed constitution. The right of the members to participate in the framing of union policies provides the basis of legitimacy.

Secrecy, kangaroo courts, private caucuses and unfair exclusions from meetings in the end represent a fundamental threat to trade unionism. Creeping apathy, poor attendances at branch meetings and increasing professionalism could, in time, erode the legitimacy of a trade union in the eyes of its members. However, the members are both the cause and the cure for the malady.

THINGS TO THINK ABOUT

Daniel Ellsberg was a top US Government researcher who 'leaked' the Pentagon Papers about the Vietnam war to the press. He claims that secrecy is a drug. People become addicted to it. Those who have access to secret information suffer from the delusion that they are superior. They think that those people who aren't in the know are fools who deserve to be manipulated because they are ignorant.

Do you find this a convincing argument? Under what circumstances, if any, should there be secret information in a voluntary organization?

7. Committees

Introduction

Committees come in all shapes and sizes, for different purposes and in different disguises. In formal organizations they are as vital as the wheel is to transport. Yet many people regard them as a curse, time-wasting, indecisive, boring, buck-passing or rubber-stamping. Committees may be unsatisfactory, but they are better than a dictatorship, which is the main alternative.

Whether you are a shop steward, a branch official, a party worker or a councillor, to be effective you have to master the art of committee work. You should know how to recognize a bad committee when you see one, even if it is only so that you can apologize and leave. Time is precious and no activist should allow any committee to waste it lightly.

Definition

What is a committee?

A committee is a purposeful gathering of a small group of people where issues are recognized and/or resolved and decisions made.

Let us look at this in detail.

Purposeful. Every member of the committee, ideally, should know why the meeting is taking place. There should also be a willingness to accept a common discipline in order to achieve a common purpose.

The gathering. A recognizable beginning and end is essential. The start should be a signal to those present that the business takes priority and that digressions and personal whims should be suppressed.

Group of people. The group should normally be three or more. (The desirable number will be discussed later.)

Issues recognized and/or resolved. This should not be confused with agreement. In some cases it may be victory merely to have the issues placed on the table and aired.

Decisions made. A committee must strive to make decisions. Once it stops striving it begins to decay. When decisions are taken they should be noted and acknowledged by all the members.

It is possible to write the specification for a bad committee. Any meeting where it is impossible to see a beginning and an end, which lacks any visible purpose, which consistently avoids issues and never knows whether it has taken a decision, reveals a rotten committee. Chairmen should remember that committees are like fish – they rot from the head down!

Size

It isn't generally realized that the size of a committee is crucially important. If you want an efficient hardworking committee with all the members playing a full part in making decisions, be sure to keep the numbers down to five, seven or nine. Six or eight member committees are equally effective *providing* a non-voting chairman is elected from the members. Otherwise, even number committees should be avoided because of the possibility of deadlock.

When setting up a committee two questions must be asked. First, how long will it last? Second, how much work will it deal with? Obviously, time and work cannot be defined in the abstract, but will depend on the situation. If, however, the time period is long, and the work heavy, a committee of nine would be right. If the work is light and time short, then five might be the answer.

On most committees of nine or more you will discover that seven people are doing the work. The rest will be passengers slowing the business down by making interjections to justify their presence. Sometimes the committee will divide itself between the establishment and the anti-establishment, with the two groups having fun loathing and criticizing each other. Such committees, to an outsider, have all the allure of an in-growing toenail.

When a committee is being run by three people, *beware*. It usually means that it consists of a dictator and two lieutenants! The committee is dead and is being used as a rubber stamp. This sometimes happens in local government when a council officer has his chairman and vice-chairman of committee in his pocket. The alternative to liquidating the committee in this case is to

liquidate the lieutenants. But in local politics this is often easier
said than done.

Purpose

Most committees find that it is valuable to have one person
responsible for seeing that the meeting does not lose sight of its
purpose. This person is usually designated as Chairman.

A few years ago a young activist who worked for the local
council asked me, 'Do all chairmen have to be bumptious,
bombastic bastards?' My answer was, 'No!'

At the same time, most people recognize that a tradition of long-winded, overbearing chairmanship has grown up within the trade union and political movements of this country. I believe that this tradition has a lot to answer for. For example, it is one reason, among many, why members prefer not to attend branch meetings.

How has the tradition developed? My guess is that *chairmanship* has become an end in itself. For generations tutors have schooled people in 'points of order', 'standing orders', and 'moving next business'. They have failed to recognize that *once a meeting gets bogged down in procedure it has failed.* An excessive devotion to procedure is a sure sign that a committee is avoiding issues, and evading making decisions.

A chairman's job is simple yet difficult. He has to serve the meeting by making sure that it does not lose sight of its goals. He should only exert his influence on issues which relate directly to the goals of the committee. He has to listen, help and encourage the other members to play their part. If, after a meeting, a chairman is asked, 'What were your opinions about that debate?' he should know it is praise beyond price.

Finally, it is the chairman's task to indicate when the meeting has begun, with 'Well, can we begin?' He should also indicate when it is no longer in session: 'I think that we have made as much progress as we are going to make today.'

Issues

It is the task of the secretary to keep track of the *issues* in a committee. In a hard-working committee the secretary should produce an *agenda* before the meeting, which includes the outstanding issues. He should take notes of the discussions, the resolutions and the decisions.

There is a tradition that the secretary should be the 'silent man' of the committee, scribbling and saying nothing. This is dangerous. The secretary should always be prepared to speak up and check the meaning and intention of the other members. If he fails to do this the result is a blurring of the issues and the committee becomes bogged down in detail.

He also should 'carry' the issues from one meeting to the next in the form of minutes or reports. But it is also the responsibility of the rest of the members to help and support the secretary. Members should specialize in certain issues and make their own notes to supplement those of the secretary. When the work-load on the secretary becomes too heavy the committee should delegate work to specialist members.

NOTE-TAKING AND REPORT WRITING

Most people's memories are fallible, so note-taking is essential. The basic principles are fairly simple and the techniques easily mastered with practice.

1. Divide your paper in half by drawing a line from top to bottom. Use the left-hand side of the page *only*. Leave the right-hand side blank.

2. Always note first the *speaker* and the *topic*. This is as important as anything which is said.

3. Listen and note down *key* words and phrases. Never attempt to take down exactly what is being said. That is a job for a professional shorthand writer, not an activist. The exception is motions and amendments which have to be taken down in full.

4. Learn to follow the *meaning* of an argument rather than sentences. With practice your hand will learn to take notes while your mind follows the argument. Note-taking can become as automatic as driving a car (and it is much less difficult).

5. When your notes are completed go back to the beginning *as soon as possible* and begin reading through. On the right-hand side of the page put down the points you missed, your own personal comments and indications about the emphasis and logic of the argument.

6. Finally, write a report from your notes leaving out those items which, on reflection, are not relevant. A good report should be more concise than the notes on which it was based.

7 Practise, practise, practise.

Crafty secretaries sometimes pull tricks on their committees. Look out for them. One favourite is manipulating the agenda. One story has it that the executive committee of one of Britain's biggest trade unions has never completed its business at one meeting. Certain issues are always craftily placed at the bottom of the agenda so that they will not be discussed and in order to prevent a decision being taken.

If you suspect that the agenda is being manipulated, insist that the agenda is made the first item of discussion. Make the secretary read out all the items on the agenda and, if necessary, rearrange their order.

Another dodge is to omit items of correspondence, or lose letters. The only solution is to treat these events as issues of *competence* and re-elect a new secretary. Kindness in the face of trickery is stupid.

Decisions

It is the job of all members to think about the issues which face a committee. Everyone should work towards collective decisions and collective responsibility.

Before a committee meets, *all* members should have taken some time to prepare themselves. Usually, this involves reading the minutes of the previous meeting and marking those passages which are vital. The agenda should also be studied. If necessary a motion to modify it should be raised at the start of the meeting.

If you see another member of a committee obviously reading his papers for the first time do not hesitate to remind him that he's wasting both his and *your* time.

Issues are often best raised on paper. If you can jot down five points and pass a copy around the committee, it will be more effective than fifteen minutes' talking. A short statement on paper, especially if it is typewritten, seems to have a kind of hypnotic quality. It may not clinch an argument but it always ensures that it receives full consideration.

Some committees manage to face the issues and yet fail to make decisions. In most cases this is because of a lack of solidarity and collective responsibility. What happens, often without anyone realizing it, is that the committee deteriorates into a negotiating body with two or more distinct parties. When this happens the power of the committee has usually been transferred either into the hands of the professionals or to the *opposition*, which will then foster the committee's existence.

Membership

Beware of committees made up of people from widely different educational or class backgrounds. In such a committee people are often determined to assert their individuality and emphasize differences. This they justify by references either to 'fundamental principles' or to the people they claim to represent outside the committee. The only solution is to 'lean on' them until they either conform or leave.

Another major danger to an effective committee is what Professor I. R. Janis calls 'groupthink',* that is, mutual brainwashing. Committees can become very much insulated from criticism and fresh ideas. The danger signs are when a committee begins to believe it is invulnerable, has an illusion of unanimity and has contempt for its opposition. Some members of the committee act as 'mind-guards' and stop adverse information and criticism from getting through, sometimes by sidetracking it, sometimes by direct action against the source.

An example would be a branch committee-man who 'bounces' critics at branch meetings. When this treatment is meted out by a 'clique' the rank-and-file members soon become angry.

There is no easy way to neutralize 'groupthink' once it breaks out. One solution is for rank-and-file members to assert themselves. Another is to rotate the role of 'devil's advocate' within the committee. If 'groupthink' occurs when there is one acknowledged leader it may be worth sacrificing him or her so that collective decision-making can resume.

Judging a Committee

Every effective working committee is different. I have deliberately not outlined the rules of procedure or given hints on how a chairman should control a committee. There is no shortage of

* I. R. Jarvis, *Victims of Groupthink* (Houghton Mifflin, 1973).

books providing that kind of information. A committee should not be judged on the way it follows the rules of procedure. It is its work, the issues which it tackles and its decisions that are important. And let's face it, committees made up of ramblers, mumblers, lazybones, self-indulgents and arrogant egotists represent the biggest drag on any voluntary movement. Tolerance is a virtue which should *always* be applied to the rank-and-file and *never* to the incapable committee-man.

THINGS TO DO

1. Make a chart of the important committees in your organization showing whether they are linked together and by what means.
2. List the jobs these committees could be tackling but aren't.

THINGS TO THINK ABOUT

1. There is a famous economic law which states that 'bad money drives out good money'. Do you think that bad ideas can drive out good ideas?
2. Is compromise always to be regretted?

---

8. Levers of Power

Introduction

In the first chapter I related how I was completely humiliated and demoralized at the branch meeting where I championed Tommy and Benny. Many people have had the same experience. But why does it happen? I think there are several reasons:

1. Most people cannot make a formal speech.
2. Most people cannot frame a resolution.

This is tragic because speeches and resolutions are the basic levers of organized power.

Speeches

It is always tempting at a formal meeting to attempt to project yourself not as you *are* but as you *would like to be*. Often people start using 'big' words and putting on the agony. However, there are only two groups of people who are really adept at this kind of projection. First, professional actors, who only develop this skill after a long and painful training. Second, natural con-artists who usually don't know who they are to start with.

First Rule

Be yourself.

Try to use the words and expressions you use every day. Forget about pronouncing your aitches, and avoid long words.

In debating societies the tradition has developed that a speaker is expected to cultivate a humorous detachment from his subject. Sometimes activists become infected with a weaker version of the virus and adopt a similar tone. There is only one acceptable *tone* for an activist's speech, namely complete commitment. Avoid flippancy or insincerity like the plague.

Second Rule

Limit your range of topics.

If a subject bores you or is outside your competence, keep quiet.

Don't begin speaking on anything and everything like people who have been taught 'public speaking' and are determined to practise on any occasion. Remember, once you start offering

your opinion on topics you are not really interested in, or well informed about, you have taken the first step towards becoming a *bore*.

Third Rule

Prepare your speech and be prepared.

Ask yourself, 'Why should they listen to me?' Whatever the answer is, act upon it.

When I went to the branch meeting to stop Benny and Tommy being sacked I had built up fantasies about what was going to happen. Because I was completely self-centred I forgot completely about the other people at the meeting. They were strangers. They weren't hostile, but they needed persuading about the injustice of the case. Because I was not prepared and tuned in to their wavelength I wasn't able to convince them.

Preparation means producing a full set of notes. *Never* attempt to write out a speech in full. The notes should be written in letters large enough to be read easily from a distance of six feet.

The most convenient way to organize notes is to write them on 5″ × 8″ cards which can be bought from stationers. These cards can be shuffled if you want to change the order of presentation. For a vital speech prepare two sets of notes. You will find that the discipline of thinking out two different approaches is the quickest way of mastering an argument.

A final point: never attempt to hide your notes. The obvious use of notes always adds authority to a speech.

Fourth Rule

Base your argument on verifiable facts.

Avoid overstatement, hearsay and public breast-beating.

At most trade union conferences some of the speakers mount the rostrum in a state of anxiety and attempt to clinch their arguments by hearsay, overstatement or personal emotional appeals. Inevitably they make fools of themselves. By relying on overstatement and hearsay they immediately make all the other facts in their case suspect. If they use a personal emotional appeal they switch the audience's attention from what they are saying to themselves. A natural audience reaction is 'What a funny man!' Remember that ranters usually sound as though they are struggling to convince themselves.

Every speech should be spiced with concrete examples which illustrate and bring the issues down to earth.

Fifth Rule

Vary the pace of your delivery and take advantage of natural pauses in the flow of your words.

Don't be afraid of silence. A long pause is often the most

"Jones is pitching it a little strong this time!"

effective way to emphasize a point. Done skilfully it has much more impact than repetition. Complete mastery of public speaking is linked with the slight changes in pace, the pauses and the emphasis which make the speech dramatic.

Some people are born orators, natural spellbinders who can ignore every rule in the book and still succeed. Nye Bevan was gifted in this way. He could entrance an audience because no one, least of all Bevan, knew where his speech was going to end. Everyone would be anxious and fascinated as they listened to him lisping, searching and hesitating before finally swooping onto the *right* word which expressed his meaning. Journalists will tell you that Bevan's speeches were magic. Afterwards their notebooks would reveal his lack of organization and substance, but *during* the speech they were usually carried along like everyone else. It was only when they began writing up their reports that they would realize how flimsy its foundations were.

Bevan and other born orators are the exceptions that prove the rule. For most people, speaking 'off the cuff' is a recipe for disaster because the inevitable outcome is repetition, confusion and incoherence.

Sixth Rule

Expect to be nervous: all good speakers are.

Remember the formula: first, a deep breath: second, a smile; third, talk to the people furthest from you.

Let me explain the formula for overcoming nervousness. When

you get to your feet and your mouth goes dry and panic strikes you, three simple actions can save the situation. First, take the deepest breath possible. Second, force a smile. Third, look at the people at the back of the hall and tell them, 'Well, I don't intend to take up a lot of your time.' You have started – and the chances are that you've won the people at the back onto your side.

As your speech progresses try to develop eye-contact with six or seven people in the audience. These contacts will provide your guide to the impression you are making. If panic returns, go back to addressing the 'friends' at the back of the hall – they're your lifeline.

Here is the prescription for a good speech which is given by many full-time trade union officials:

1. Tell them what you're going to say.
2. Tell them.
3. Tell them what you've just told them.

Motions

Motions are the main levers for *moving* an organization. They are essential tools, yet every union conference and every political meeting produces a crop of inadequate ones. Many motions are badly constructed: too long, too short, too sharp, too blunt or too twisted. However, it is *easy* for any activist to create an effective and hard-hitting motion if he follows a few simple rules.

Trial Balloons and Action

There are two different jobs you can do with motions. First, you can use a motion to *test* whether the organization is ready to start moving in a certain direction. This is called a *trial balloon*. Secondly, you can use it to call for changes, for movement to begin. This is a *call for action*.

A trial balloon asks the membership to accept an opinion or an attitude. Here's an example from a recent Trades Union Congress:

> Congress deplores the fact that in times of economic stringency Governments rush to impose arbitrary staff cuts on the Civil Service. Congress believes this is a short-sighted practice which not only prevents an improvement in services to the public but also produces a deterioration in the quality of existing services, particularly in the field of social welfare.

The proposers of the motion are asking their fellow delegates to agree with them. They do not suggest that anyone should take any action to stop the Government cutting back the staff of the Civil Service. Compare the trial balloon with this call for action which was proposed at the same Congress:

> Congress is concerned that acts of suppression against workers and trade unionists by totalitarian regimes, to prevent an extension of the free trade union movement, are continuing.

> Congress again, therefore, declares its determination towards the achievement of world-wide free trade unions and expresses its solidarity for the right of peoples to organise free trade unions, free speech and assembly, free and democratic elections, by reaffirming total opposition to imprisonment without trial or by secret and military courts.

> Congress, in support of these aims, calls upon the General Council to render assistance wherever possible to bring to fruition the right that all peoples of all lands shall live in freedom.

The call for action in this long and rather wordy resolution asks the 'General Council to render assistance', which is a fairly vague requirement. The resolution could have been more specific. But the more detailed a call for action becomes the more it ties the hands of the professionals who have to implement it. And most professionals prefer flexibility and room to manoeuvre.

Constructing a Motion

A good motion should be self-contained. It should include all the necessary information to make up either a trial balloon or a call for action.

The following three steps are the specification for a trial balloon motion.

1. It should *identify* the motion's sponsors.
2. It should explain *why* the motion is necessary.
3. It should *declare* the appropriate attitude or opinion.

Another two steps are needed to make a call for action.

4. It must be decided *who* should take action.
5. It must be decided *what* action should be taken and when.

With a *call for action* motion step (3) can sometimes be dropped, especially if it is likely to provoke heated opposition. Remember the ultimate goal is to get the organization moving, not to play an elaborate game of scoring points over the opposition.

Example   The following motion uses all the steps from (1) to (5).

(1) This branch (2) having been messed about for twelve months by head office (3) declares that the situation is now intolerable and (4) calls on the General Secretary as the person mainly responsible (5) to resign immediately.

Amendments

Amendments can be thought of as small wedges driven in behind the lever of a motion in order to change the direction of movement. They are not levers themselves. Amendments work by adding or deleting words from the original motion. There are three essential steps:

1. *Specify* whether words are added or deleted.

2. State *where* the change should occur.
3. *Spell out* the exact wording of the change.

Example   Let us amend the motion which calls for the resignation of the General Secretary. If one person feels that the situation was not so much intolerable as typical, the following amendment might be proposed: '(1) *Delete* after (2) "head office" the words "declares that the situation is now intolerable".' Because the amendment neither distorts nor contradicts the original motion the Chairman of the meeting would be obliged to accept it.

However, someone else might feel that more than the General Secretary should be purged. A second amendment might read:

'(1) *Delete* after (2) "General Secretary" the words "as the person mainly responsible" and (2) *add* in their place the words (3) "and the Executive Committee as the people responsible".'

It is normal practice for the last amendment to be put first to the vote. As the amendments are accepted they become incorporated into the composite motion which *must* be put to the meeting for a final deciding vote. It is not uncommon for this vital final step to be overlooked. Remember the rule: *only one amendment at a time*.

Resolutions

A resolution is a motion which has been moved, seconded and approved by a meeting. What began as a lever in the hands of an activist becomes a movement within the organization. Remember, though, that resolutions need to be followed through. Sometimes the professionals try to block a motion, or if this fails, they will overtly accept the decision – and then allow it to die from neglect. This can happen in most voluntary organizations. Resolutions need as much pushing as an original motion, and sometimes more.

THINGS TO DO

1. Convert the Civil Service *trial balloon* motion on page 69 into a *call for action*.
2. Rewrite the 'freedom' motion to the General Council in two short sentences.

Section IV 'Don't Quote Me . . .'

We have looked at the activist's role in informal situations and in formal organizations. In this final section we look at the activist and the mass media, that is, newspapers and other sorts of news.

The press, radio and television provide spectators, outsiders, members and activists with information and tailor-made attitudes. They supply some of the topics for day-to-day conversation on the shop floor, in the home and in the pub. The media offer an agenda of what they consider to be significant and important in society. In the long term this agenda must, inevitably, become a powerful conditioning force within a society.

But the press and broadcasting also offer opportunities to the activist. In the right situation they are an efficient means of communicating with members. They are an important method of educating and informing the general public.

All activists have a vested interest in the fullest, most free flow of information within their organization and in society at large. Voluntary organizations, because they are 'open' public bodies, depend on fresh reliable information to make sense of their environment and also to develop effective strategies. Secrecy and misinformation are the weapons of the vested interests who oppose and try to 'con' trade unions, political parties and community groups. In the final analysis, voluntary organizations are the natural allies of the investigative journalist and the crusading editor. Their demand must always be for more disclosure, never less.

This section, therefore, is concerned with three related topics. First, an outline of the traditions and the methods of organization of the press. Secondly, notes on how to establish a friendly working relationship with your local newspaper. Thirdly, a description of some of the problems that can crop up in television and radio.

9. News Organizations

Introduction

News-gathering and publishing in Britain is a complex business. There is a widespread delusion that the nine daily and seven Sunday national newspapers, together with the output of ITV and BBC, comprise the only significant area of journalism. In fact, they are merely the tip of the iceberg. There are over one hundred provincial daily papers and more than one thousand local papers published every week. It is a sobering thought to realize that the births, marriages and deaths columns of the local newspaper are probably read with closer interest in your community by more people than read the editorials of the *Guardian*, the *Daily Telegraph*, the *Times* and the *Financial Times* put together.

The national news organizations feed on the stories of the provincial press. In every newspaper office there are people clipping stories out of other newspapers which will either be followed up and developed or filed in the cuttings library for future reference. The reporters on the local paper probably make a few pounds, on the side, by sending 'copy' to Fleet Street. In some parts of the country, journalists working for different papers operate a 'ring' for sharing stories with each other. In these and other ways the whole news-gathering system is linked together.

But before outlining the way news operations are organized it is useful to see the traditions of the British press in their social and historical perspective. Pontificating editors like to claim that the press is the watchdog of the public interest. Their critics (journalists among them) often retort that they are merely the lapdogs of the vested interest. The truth probably lies somewhere in between.

Traditions

The press in Britain has never had control over its own destiny. Over the years three powerful forces have helped to shape it: first, the Government; secondly, finance and industry; and thirdly, the link between mass circulation and advertising.

The tradition of British government has its roots in the arrogant, aristocratic, anti-democratic ruling élites of previous centuries who despised and opposed the press. One of the enduring articles of faith of élitism is that key information should remain within the 'charmed circle'. This tradition lingers on. Knowledge is the currency of power and all governments eventually become misers. But the inbuilt secrecy of governments has multiplied as the Civil Service has expanded. And bureaucrats have their own reasons for hiding from the public. So throughout the twentieth century legal restrictions on the free flow of information have spread like the tentacles of an octopus.

Today, anything which could be embarrassing or damaging to the Government or the Civil Service is liable to become a classified secret. In fact, we have had top civil servants refusing to reveal to elected Members of Parliament vital information about Concorde and blatantly admitting that they would *deliberately* cook the books to hide facts!

Journalists sometimes refer to real news, by which they mean something that someone doesn't want to see published. Governments control real news, but they compensate by having publicity mills in Whitehall which specialize in stuffing the mass media with pseudo-news, information that they want to be put across to the public. Unfortunately, the press has learned not to bite the hand that force-feeds it!

The second powerful influence on the press has been finance and industry. To a businessman or financier 'information' often means an opportunity for financial gain. So secrecy and deliberate misinformation have become a way of life in industrial and financial affairs. As Robert Townsend, former Chairman of Avis Rent-a-Car, phrased it: 'All the big company managements I am familiar with are basically engaged (whether they are conscious of it or not) in screwing their stockholders, employees, customers, and the general public as well, while living off the fat of the land themselves.'*

Understandably, management prefer to do their screwing behind closed doors. It takes a merger, a directors' quarrel or a bankruptcy to reveal all the hidden 'strokes' being pulled in the

* The Ups and Downs of Working Life', in *Center* magazine, January–February 1972.

board room and by the higher echelons of management. Industry handles the press in the same way as Government: it starves it of real news and force-feeds it with pseudo-news. Many a lavish public relations luncheon is followed by a regurgitation of favourable 'facts' in the next edition.

Advertising and mass circulation have also shaped the role, the style and the economics of the press. According to two Royal Commissions, advertisers here don't stand behind the editor's chair calling the shots. It is as well they don't. When the advertising agencies in the United States controlled network broadcasting they were ruthless censors. Camel cigarettes sponsored a news programme, but they banned all films which showed people smoking cigars (with the sole exception of Winston Churchill)! They sponsored plays in which the villain was forbidden to smoke. Their scriptwriters could never mention a fire because the viewer might connect fires with cigarettes. In Britain, advertiser boycotts are not unknown, though the press is very reluctant to reveal them. So we do not know the extent of direct influence by advertisers on the press. It is the indirect influence of advertising which has been (and still is) tremendous, especially in the 'light' papers, the *Mail*, *Mirror*, *Sun* and *Express*. Increased circulation inevitably attracts more advertising revenue. Advertisers are interested in buying the attention of the maximum number of people for the lowest possible cost. Papers with the largest circulations can charge very high advertising rates and yet still offer a lower cost per thousand than its rivals. Success breeds success. Even though 1,250,000 readers were pleased to buy the *News Chronicle*, a fantastic number of people by any standard, the owners still closed it down for lack of advertiser support.

Advertising is the main financial support of the press in this country. Without advertising, the price of the *Daily Mirror* would increase fourfold and the *Daily Telegraph* would rise eightfold – *assuming they did not lose any readers*. Probably a ban on advertising would multiply the price by ten and divide the circulation by a similar amount. Are we to believe that editors *never* reflect that the fortunes of their paper and the advertising industry are inextricably linked?

The search for the biggest possible circulation has affected the whole approach and style of the 'light' papers. And where they have led, the 'heavy' papers and the provincial press have tended to follow. The 'light' papers have competed with each other by mixing entertainment with news. They all search constantly for human interest stories, gossip, crime, sexual shenanigans and a constantly updated service for students of form, both sporting and female. The reports of the Profumo and Lambton affairs are remembered as 'cracking good political stories', which is an indication of the strength and weakness of the 'light' papers.

To be fair, I should point out that some editors of the 'light' papers have attempted to educate their readers in a very capable and entertaining way. They have employed the finest journalists in the country, men and women who have mastered the difficult art of crisp direct writing. Any activist who wants a model to improve his ability to express himself in writing need look no further than the *Daily Mirror*.

In summary, British news organizations reflect the society in which they have developed. Of course, provincial papers, especially the weeklies, haven't been influenced by the Government as much as the national papers. But the provincial press is, if anything, more subject to the influence of local industrialists and key advertisers. And with the continual development of local news monopolies this kind of influence becomes doubly dangerous.

Manufacturing the News

Many people think that news must have a special ingredient. This is wrong. Most news is manufactured. The amount of news in your town or city depends *not* so much on what is happening but more on the energy and imagination of the local journalists. In the North of England there are two very similar cities founded on former Roman settlements. In one, a vigorous press agency pours out stories to the national newspapers, to radio and to television. Editors see it as a vital interesting city. The other city probably contains more stories, but they are never discovered. So the second city is classed as a quaint backwater.

News-gathering has to be organized. A local press agency has to *sell* stories to survive. A newspaper reporter has to bring back stories to keep his job. An editor cannot afford to send reporters on too many wild-goose chases. A producer does not want to waste the time of a film crew and film, on an uninteresting event. The pages must be filled and the programmes must appear. The system cannot and dare not admit that there is no news today. In fact, there is always news around; the problem is finding it.

Let me tell you how it is done. Every serious news organization depends on its diary and its contacts. The diary contains details of all predicted and expected events. I have met scores of activists who have complained that the press did not turn up to cover an event or a demonstration. My first question is always, 'Did you give them adequate advance warning?' If they haven't then they can only blame themselves, not the press. Newspapers, press agencies and freelancers rely on their contacts. If it appears to be a thin day for news journalists begin ringing round their contacts. Policemen, businessmen, trade union leaders, doctors, publicans, politicians, teachers, convenors are all featured in a good journalist's contact book. Some people in key jobs – motorway ambulance drivers, for example – are 'tipsters' and are paid a few pounds every time they phone in a lead to a story. So the news-gathering system relies on a network of contacts distributed through society.

The diary, tips, leads and the daily prospect sheet from the Press Association guide an editor in allocating jobs to his reporters and stringers. Some assignments are given a day in advance.

The first important event in the day of a newspaper is the *morning conference*. The details vary in different organizations, but the conference is a meeting of the Editor with his news, sport, city, features and other departmental editors to review the prospects for the day. At this meeting they agree on the 'shape' of the paper or the programme for that day. Each of the departmental heads tries to 'sell' certain items to the editor; they compete with each other in claiming space. At these conferences a *story-line* is often hammered out. For example, if a strike has been running for six weeks the editor might 'buy' a story that concentrates on the hardship suffered by the strikers' wives and children. Or if the other news organizations have given treatment to a celebrity of the moment the conference might agree to 'look at a knocking piece'. In other words, they might

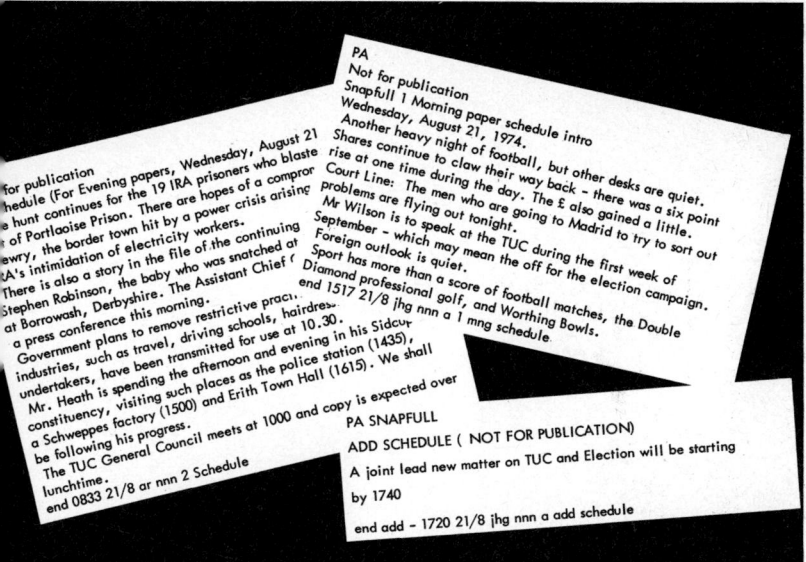

The Press Association's early warning schedule

commission a story which will challenge the image of the man without necessarily committing themselves to publish or broadcast it.

After the morning conference the departmental editor may give the reporter an explicit definition of what the story is about, or he may leave the reporter free to write the story in the most relevant and interesting way he thinks possible.

When an activist meets a reporter on an assignment he should try to discover what this prior definition of the story is. It only needs a simple question: 'Tell me, before I answer your question, what do you think this story is about?' If the reporter cannot or will not answer, give him the bum's rush!

Most reporters will respond, because they have a threefold job to do. First, they have to gather the available facts of the story. Secondly, they have to check the facts to the best of their ability. And thirdly, they have to check the story-line. If they discover that their editor's directive about the story is wrong it

Journalists cover the press conference

Phoning in the story

Copy tasting and spiking

```
PA Snapfull
1 TUC
WILSON FOR TUC CONGRESS
By Charles Goodson, the PA Industrial Correspondent.
  The General Council of the TUC today decided to invite the Prime Minister to
address the TUC annual congress at Brighton during the first week in September.
  This would give Mr Wilson the opportunity, if he wishes, to use the TUC as a
launching pad for an election campaign, although Mr Len Murray, TUC General
Secretary, denied this was the purpose of the invitation.
  "That was not in our minds at all," he said.
MF 21/8 1238 AR nnn 1 tuc
```

Taking copy

Sub-editing the copy

Copy on the wire

Into the early editions

will save them a great deal of time and energy. But this precon-
ception about a story can only be refuted by *facts*; an alternative story-line needs evidence to support it.

The activist has his first, last and only chance of deciding
what the story will be when he talks to the reporter, for once it
has been sent into the news room it becomes part of a pro-
cessing system.

A vast flood of paper from staff reporters, specialist correspondents, news agencies and stringers around the country
deluges into newspaper and broadcasting news rooms. Before
any story is presented to the public it has to clear a series of
hurdles. A 'copy-taster' is the first journalist to examine material
sent in for publication. If he thinks that the story does not
'make', then it is dead. If he accepts the story it is passed on to
a sub-editor who corrects it, alters it to match the overall style
of the paper, gives it headlines and subheadings, and sometimes rewrites the opening paragraph or the whole piece.
Finally, the copy is marked up for printing.

Then it is passed on to the Chief Sub-Editor for his scrutiny.
He may consult his specialist correspondent (see Box on page
83) who provides news, background information and guidance
within his sphere of responsibility. The specialist's comments
may 'kill' the story because it is wrong, mischievous, or prema-
ture. If the story clears this hurdle it passes into the composing
room to be cast into columns of type. But it still has a couple of
hurdles to cross. The proof copy is examined by a legal expert
who may 'kill' it. Then departmental editors and proof-readers
cast their critical eye over the story before it goes on to the
complete page together with pictures and advertising. This takes
time and journalists have to learn to work under pressure.

The same kind of editing and rewriting takes place in radio
and in television, where the process is more complicated because
news programmes contain films and videotapes as well as
written scripts.

Deadlines are the very heart of a news organization. Many a
good story has been lost through arriving after a deadline. An
out-of-date story is as dead as a dodo.

One way the press can be manipulated is to release a story
deliberately so late in the day that it is impossible for a journalist to check it out. He cannot find anyone to offer a counter-

SPECIALIST CORRESPONDENTS AND ACTIVISTS

'Specialist correspondents spend their first two years enthusiastically chasing their own stories and the next twenty years killing other people's.'

News Editor.

Industrial and political correspondents spend their time talking to and relating to *professionals*. They develop an extremely stereotyped and distorted view of the role and work of the *activists*. From the vantage point of trade union and political conferences activists seem to be either *loyal* or *disloyal* troops.

Industrial correspondents are usually sympathetic to trade unions. But many of them spend their time reporting those rituals of confrontation that take place in London. Much of the industrial reporting in the rest of the country falls into the hands of non-specialists. An activist, therefore, should *never* assume that a general reporter, freelance or agency man has any insight or grasp of an industrial story. All journalists should be *educated* into the realities of the story.

vailing opinion. Then if it is a dramatic event the editors are faced with a dilemma. Should they publish the story hedged round with qualifications which would destroy its impact? Should they insert a final paragraph which expresses their doubt? Should they leave it till the next day and risk their rivals stealing a march on them? In this sort of crisis the papers, the BBC and ITV are liable to make gross editorial errors. These are understandable but can never be excused.

Conclusion

This chapter has provided a sketch of news organizations in Britain, an attempt to show them operating in a social environment. It must be recognized that for many voluntary organizations the press is a convenient and complacent scapegoat. The activist who exclaims, 'We never get a fair press!' is right. But no organization *consistently* gets a fair press. Most politicians and industrialists will testify that a honeymoon period with the British press is invariably short and ends with mutual recriminations.

Trade unions and political parties sometimes confuse their own real crises with the press crises which follow. In the inquests the shadows which have flickered through the media are sometimes confused with the substance of the real issues. And it is so easy to attack the press, if only because its faults are revealed daily. The press is no better and no worse than the society in which it operates. An activist should draw a clear distinction between the press as a whole and an individual reporter.

An activist should always be prepared to meet on an equal basis the reporter who is gathering the facts of a story. The latter is a worker trying to do his job. The former is a trade unionist who does not control the industry in which he works. Both have a vested interest in more information, in greater disclosure and in less secrecy. If they can form an understanding and an alliance they could benefit each other.

THINGS TO DO

1. Make a list of the topics you find interesting and which should be covered by a good newspaper.
2. Buy some newspapers and mark the stories which cover your selected topics.
3. Take a ruler and measure the number of column inches for each of these.
4. Make a bar chart which shows the column inches for each topic in the different newspapers.

This picture expresses the growing militancy of civil servants in a way that no writer could put into words

10. Making an Impression

Introduction

Few voluntary organizations can afford to disregard any means of communicating with their members or the general public. The easiest, quickest and simplest method available to an activist, a branch, a committee, or an organization is through a local newspaper or radio station. Of course, it is no use rushing down to the local newspaper office with a manifesto of 3,000 words on how you intend to change the world. The only sure way of making an impression in the local press is by developing a friendly relationship with the journalists. But first an activist has to build up his own confidence in handling stories. Then he must give the journalists time to learn to have confidence in him.

Basic Strategy

A crisis situation or a conflict story, which always draw reporters like bees to honey, is the most *unfavourable* setting in which to establish a relationship.

Begin when things are quiet. Study the kind of stories that appear in the local press. You will find that many of them are simple human interest stories. Local papers tend to be filled with more 'good' news than the national papers. Usually there's a story about a local boy or girl, complete with photograph, who is serving abroad in the armed forces. In fact, the Army has supplied the newspaper with that story for nothing. Why? Simply because it helps the Army with recruitment. And the paper publishes it because it *is* local news.

A trade union branch is full of people leading interesting, eventful lives. The union's solicitors may win an insurance claim for a member. Someone else may receive a book grant for a son or daughter at college. A shop steward joins a delegation to Germany. The Branch Chairman flies to Canada to see his long-lost brother. All of them are interesting events though, let's face it, none of them are going to shake the world. But there are very many of these stories and most local papers will be very pleased to know about them.

If every local newspaper carried stories showing trade unionists leading rich, full, rewarding lives, and deriving practical benefits from being trade union members, the public image of trade unions would improve.

To 'place' such stories does not involve 'conning' the local press. These stories are real and happen every day of the week and they are not published because trade unionists do not take the steps to see that they are reported.

Obviously, it is unwise for the activist to approach the local paper off his own bat. A collective decision is needed from the branch or the executive committee. But once there is agreement on a policy for improving relations with the press, the activist can begin a serious strategy.

Preparation

For a few weeks try to discover human interest stories about members. Note them down and save them. At the same time begin researching the local news situation. Go to the local library and ask for two books: the *Newspaper Press Directory* and the *World's Press News Directory of Newspaper and Magazine Personnel and Data*. From these you should be able to discover a lot of information. Have a chat with the librarian about the local press. Librarians are a mine of information.

Make a note of when the local paper is published. Try to find out when it goes to press, the last day and time for receiving news and the best day for submitting news. Each will be a different day. For example, the best day to send news to a weekly paper which is delivered to your house on a Friday may be Monday. On Tuesday the paper will begin to be made up. On Wednesday it will be set and the proofs read, and on Thursday it will be printed and delivered to the newsagent. These are the key deadlines so it is important to know them.

Contact

Find out which reporter specializes in industrial stories, ring him up, and suggest a meeting. By this time you will know who owns the paper, whether it is part of a group, who is the editor, and the size and distribution of the circulation. When you meet the reporter be frank. Tell him that you want to improve relations and that you are speaking for your branch and your colleagues. Ask him about the paper and the way it is organized. Because you have done your homework digging out the facts, the reporter will quickly recognize that you are serious and competent. The most difficult job has been done. You have established your credibility!

Mention the stories you have collected and ask whether he finds them interesting. With any luck the reporter may follow one of them up. Certainly, you'll be questioned about future prospects. The success of the meeting can be judged in two ways. First, the reporter should put your name, address and telephone number in his contacts book. Second, you should discover the best method and time to submit news to the paper. The reporter might prefer you to give him a ring, or he might want something on paper sent into the office. Either way, accept his advice and guidance and follow it to the letter.

Routine

Make the press relations exercise a team effort with everyone in the branch making a contribution. Every week, on the appropriate day, try to send at least one item of news to the paper. Not everything will find its way into print but you will become established as a regular reliable source. Buy two copies of the paper and clip any stories that appear. Paste one clipping into a large cuttings book which forms your record. The other can be placed on a union notice board or somewhere where the members can read it.

Once you have set up this basic routine it should be possible to branch out. Make contact with other members of the editorial staff and reporters working for the local press agency. Consider inviting the local editor along to the branch meeting. Most editors are prepared to talk about their views of the problems and the prospects of the local community. If the editor prefers to spend his time at the local golf club, or with the Rotarians, invite his assistant editor or senior reporter instead. Remember the press depends on its personal contact with people, and that trade unions, political parties and community groups are made up of people and, most importantly, of readers.

Development

Once good relations have been established you are in a strong position if and when trouble blows up. If a strike or a work-to-rule develops the local journalists will know *where* and *how* to check any press releases from the company's public relations officer. If a London reporter comes to cover the story the local press agency will guide him in your direction. Of course, there is no guarantee of fair treatment, but at least you will have a chance to tell your story.

On and Off the Record

Journalists work to a strict code of conduct which says:

A journalist should fully realise his personal responsibility for everything he sends to his paper or agency. He should keep union and professional secrets, and respect all necessary confidences regarding sources of information and private documents. He should not falsify information or documents, or distort or misrepresent facts.*

Both you and the journalist should understand clearly whether a statement you give is *on* the record or *off* the record. If you privately supply him with background information and some important implications of a story, it is usually *off the record.* You can expect your identity not to be revealed. On the other hand, if you say, 'You can quote me on this,' you are on the record. You should never give information to a journalist and then ask him not to use it. Journalists are prepared to use discretion and protect their sources but they are unwilling to *suppress* information.

This problem does not occur in a face-to-face situation. It is the telephone that causes misunderstandings – and the telephone is the journalist's major working tool. Many people become casual and sloppy when they use a telephone. Otherwise cautious people make indiscreet and wild statements. If you are wise, treat every telephone interview with great caution.

* National Union of Journalists' Code of Conduct.

Planning a Campaign

Sometimes trade union branches, political parties and community groups decide to hold a campaign and try to draw the local press into it. It may be about bad working conditions, a pedestrian subway or a kiddies' playground. I have seen scores of campaigns fizzle out in a fortnight because activists expect results too quickly. So here are a few guidelines for would-be campaigners:

1. Expect to spend at least two months on the campaign. If the issue isn't worth two months' work then it isn't a campaigning issue.
2. Expect the local press to be sceptical at first. Remember these journalists have to listen to the grinding of axes every week.
3. You will need people and events. Both will have to be organized. Petitions, delegations, marches, demonstrations and picketing are the kind of events which are always newsworthy.
4. Before every event make sure that the local press is informed of (a) its purpose, (b) who the opposition is, (c) how many people will be taking part (and point out that they read the newspaper), (d) *who* the reporter *and photographer* should contact, *where* and at *what time*.
5. If you are attempting an exposé of bad working conditions or a slum school, it is important to get the evidence – photographs and statements – *before* the campaign starts.
6. Don't throw your best ammunition away at the beginning of the campaign. Try timing the 'events' so that the pressure builds up.
7. Don't *start* a debate in the correspondence columns of the local press. If your campaign is effective, *someone* somewhere is bound to attack you. Then reply.
8. Watch out for professional band-wagon riders. They may join you for their own purposes and sell the issue down the river.

Don't be afraid to break off the interview in order to prepare yourself and gather the facts and arguments you need. And always indicate when you are *on* and *off* the record.

Six Important Do's and Don't's

When dealing with a journalist:

ALWAYS
1. Be truthful.
2. Be friendly.
3. Be accessible.

NEVER
4. Begrudge assistance.
5. Try to block a story without countervailing evidence.
6. Waste time when a journalist is striving to meet a deadline.

---

11. Broadcasting

Introduction

Broadcasting is a boon to the activist. It allows him to express his personal point of view first hand, without rewrites or misleading headlines. But radio and television have their own technical and operational limitations and the activist should be aware of them.

Limitations

Radio and television are excellent at conveying human emotions, but they are less successful at analysing news or ideas in depth. There just isn't enough time to do it properly. There are more words in this book than will be used on the 'News at Ten' in a week! An 'in depth' analysis on television or radio needs at least forty-five minutes – and even then the surface will be little more than scratched.

Tampering with the Tape

Many interviews are recorded. Activists fear that producers will deliberately edit tape in order to distort or reverse their arguments. In fact, this rarely *if ever* happens; it is more than a producer's job is worth. In any case, editing is a chore that most television and radio producers try to avoid at all costs. If they can obtain a clear concise interesting interview they are delighted to leave it as it is. Producers will only, in fact, edit in order to fit an interview into a time slot, to remove irrelevancies, repetition and confusion. Their personal whims and biases are usually reflected in the people they choose to interview and the material they reject out-of-hand.

Live Televised Discussions

A much more serious form of distortion arises when a group of activists confront a couple of professionals in a live TV programme. These situations are dynamite. Usually, the activists emerge as an undisciplined rabble. In contrast, the professionals are portrayed as cool, calm and reasonable.

Let me tell you how it happens. Usually the producer fails to allocate enough time to the discussion. As a rough guide there should be at least two minutes for everyone taking part. Less time means that people have been brought into the studio to be part of the scenery.

The professionals sit at table with their own individual microphones. (The symbolic significance of the table as a barrier is not lost on the viewers.) The activists usually sit on a tier of benches. What the viewer cannot see is the man off-camera with a boom who operates a microphone above the heads of the group. Of course, the activists see it and keep watching it like a tempting bait.

When the programme starts the activists are excited. They listen to the professionals' case – which is presented quietly and reasonably. By the time the activists join in the pressure is on.

Bill Grundy is an expert at getting people to be themselves in a television studio but the man on the boom microphone has a power that the viewer never sees

They have to compete for the microphone dangling above their heads – and he who shouts loudest usually wins. The others begin interrupting him and each other. All the viewer sees is a jostling, argumentative rabble snatching at questions like hungry seals being fed at the zoo.

Finally, the interviewer will bring the discussion back to the professionals who make their points on their individual microphones. The activists can be ignored now because the interviewer knows that the boom microphone has been silenced by the engineer in the cubicle. Once the programme is finished the producer will smooth the activists' ruffled feelings, confident that he has given the viewers what he thinks they want – a verbal punch-up.

Why do activists go into the studios? In most cases, trade unionists venture into this strange territory in order to convey solidarity, unity and determination. But if this is their intention they usually fail miserably.

What is the alternative? The best advice is to treat a studio situation like a negotiation. Elect a couple of spokesmen. If there is only four minutes for discussion elect no more than two speakers. In the studio the rest of the group should confine themselves to supporting, amplifying and applauding the statements of their spokesmen.

On most programmes the interviewer likes a preliminary chat with the people he is going to talk to. Usually this provides an opportunity for him to outline the key questions and the way the topic is going to be treated. If you think that a distorted line is being taken you should say so as soon as possible and back up your argument with all the facts at your command. If the interviewer will not change his tack, you should try your damnedest to expose him during the programme, citing chapter and verse.

It is ridiculously easy to begin a counter-attack. You simply say, 'Why do you ask that question?' Once the interviewer has completed his explanation (and most of them will be taken aback) you can move in and take over the discussion. Probably, you will never appear on that programme again, but at least you will have made your point.

Filmed Interviews

The problem that film crews have with an interview is how to photograph two faces with one camera. They start by aiming the camera at the person answering the questions. Then, when the interview is complete, they move the camera to another spot and film the interviewer doing 'cut-aways' and repeating his questions. Cut-aways are short lengths of film with the interviewer nodding and smiling. These are used to bridge the gaps when the film is edited together in the cutting room.

Interviewers usually look funny or ridiculous gazing into space smiling and nodding and saying, 'And tell me, Mr Jones, is it true . . .?' Because they look ridiculous they prefer the person they have been talking to not to be around. My advice is, if you have been interviewed, stay around, not for a laugh but to listen to the questions repeated. Sometimes the questions when repeated are slightly modified because the interviewer is constantly tempted to 'improve' on his question the second time round. Your presence will curb his temptation. If you hear a question being wrongly repeated your best protection is to shout Eric Morecambe's catch phrase 'Rubbish' in a loud voice. This will ruin the soundtrack on the 'take' and put you in a strong position when you are arguing about what the *right* question should be.

Protection

If you decide for one reason or another that you do not want your film or radio interview broadcast, you must *immediately* tell the interviewer. Find out from him who is the producer of the programme and telephone as soon as possible to say that the interview must not be broadcast. (Remember you cannot do this with a newspaper!) Insist that a note is taken of the time and date of your objection. Of course, the producer may decide to broadcast and be damned. The only remaining remedy then is the courts.

Obviously, it is far better not to consent to a dodgy interview in the first place. Remember always to check the story-line with the interviewer before agreeing to talk to him!

THINGS TO DO

1. Watch your local regional news programme and count the number of cut-aways in the filmed interviews.
2. Watch for group discussions on the national current affairs programmes. Time the discussions and count the people involved. Work out how much time *should* have been given to the discussion.

Postscript

I hope you have found the first reading of this handbook valuable and rewarding. Some of it may not seem terribly relevant to your situation. Some of the ideas and some of the problems we have been looking at may seem strange or unusual. This is to be expected. If we were to sit down together and rewrite the handbook, I am sure there are a lot of things we would want to change.

So where do *you* go from here? May I suggest that you start making your own Activist's Handbook? You can start with the exercises that appear at the end of the chapters. You can go on to cover those topics I have neglected.

But keep this little book handy. It is meant to cast light on a number of problems. I hope that you are going to find it useful in the future.

Illustration Acknowledgements

Associated Newspapers page 48; Nick Birch page 80; Camera Press page 70; Central Press page 84; Ron Chapman page 41; Euan Duff page 33; Mark Edwards (bottom right photo) page 80; Neil Gulliver pages 40–1; Larry Herman page 40; Bob Houlton pages 6, 25, 57; Bill Leimbach page 40; Angela Phillips page 40; Press Association pages 79, 80; Press Association Photos page 72; Colin Smithson pages 20–1, 63–7; *Punch* pages 16–7; Chris Steele-Perkins pages 40–1; Thames Television page 92; Topix page 40; TUC page 48; John Walmsley pages 41, 48; Patrick Ward page 41

If you would like a descriptive list of the other books in the Trade Union Industrial Studies series published by Arrow Books please send a postcard to P.O. Box 29, Douglas, Isle of Man, Great Britain.